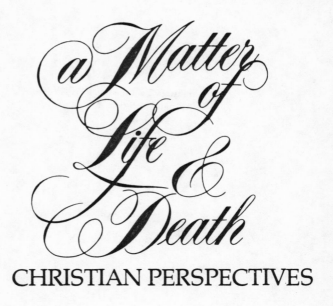

a Matter of Life & Death

CHRISTIAN PERSPECTIVES

Compiler/Contributor

Harry Hollis

Broadman Press
Nashville, Tennessee

© Copyright 1977 • Broadman Press
All rights reserved.
4261-18
ISBN: 0-8054-6118-3

Dewey Decimal Classification: 241
Subject heading: CHRISTIAN ETHICS

Library of Congress Catalog Card Number: 76-058207
Printed in the United States of America.

Preface

When I came to this conference on biomedical ethics, I thought we would be dealing with theoretical matters far removed from my everyday experience. But, I have just learned that I must go to the hospital to help a family decide whether to have surgery performed on their baby, whom the doctors say is going to die in a few days no matter what medical procedure is followed. And now I realize how important it is to study and think about these issues. Right now I need help in deciding what to do.

These words were spoken by a pastor who attended the Christian Life Commission conference on biomedical ethics last year. His dilemma points to a problem that many of us face about biomedical issues. We come up against practical situations about which we must make moral decisions; yet we have not been adequately prepared to make these decisions. We have not received adequate biblical, theological, or scientific information to help us decide about biomedical issues.

The chapters of this book have been written by people who made presentations at the Christian Life Commission Biomedical Ethics Conference. This conference brought together lay people and professionals, young and old, physicians and theologians, scientists and pastors, to listen and to discuss such issues as biomedical decision making, euthanasia, behavior control, abortion, human experimentation, genetic engineering, and related matters which require moral decisions. People from fifteen states attended the conference which was held at the Southern Baptist Convention Building in Nashville.

This book has been written by people who are involved in biomedical decision making. They are active in the fields of religion and medicine. They write from a Christian perspective. They are involved in professions that deal with biomedical decisions.

It is the hope of these writers and of the Christian Life Commission that this book will be a helpful resource in preparation for decisions about biomedical issues.

Dr. Foy Valentine has headed the Southern Baptist Christian Life Commission for more than fifteen years. During that time he has given matchless leadership in bringing the moral word of the gospel to bear on the problems that Christians must face in society. Foy Valentine is an unselfish enabler who assists his own staff in writing and speaking on moral concerns. I am especially grateful to him for his encouragement and advice about conducting the biomedical ethics conference and about completing this book. I am also grateful to my colleagues at the Christian Life Commission, Floyd Craig, Welton Gaddy, David Sapp, and John Wood, for their valuable help.

To Miss Mary Elizabeth Tyler, I express appreciation for her tireless labor in overseeing the typing and assembly of this book. Ms. Faye Russell and Mrs. Annette Hayward typed the chapters with skill and patience.

Dag Hammarskjold once said that "the road to holiness passes through the world of action." Believing this to be true, this book is offered in the strong conviction that Christians must be actively involved in the world of biomedical issues. It is the deep hope of the writers that this book will prompt intelligent and responsible involvement.

Harry N. Hollis, Jr.
February 1, 1977

Contents

1
Biomedical Ethics:
An Overview
Harry N. Hollis, Jr.

In this introductory chapter, the compiler underscores the central idea of the study. Christianity is relevant to biomedical ethics and provides both wisdom and motivation to deal with these issues.

The need for dialogue between science and religion is stressed and the purposes of the book are set forth. Attention is given to the task of the Christian ethicist in relation to biomedical issues, and the sources of ethical insights are discussed.

One possible theological model for use in considering biomedical issues is sketched. The heart of this model is the biblical teaching that God is active in the world as Creator, Judge, and Redeemer; and human beings are called to respond to what he is doing.

Harry Hollis Jr. is a staff member of the Southern Baptist Christian Life Commission where he serves as Director of Family and Special Moral Concerns. Before coming to his present position, he served as a pastor in Kentucky and taught Christian Ethics at Southern Baptist Theological Seminary. He has previously written *The Shoot-'Em-Up Society* and *Thank God for Sex!*, and he was compiler/contributor of *Christian Freedom for Women and Other Human Beings*.

Biomedical Ethics:
An Overview

While health is not the totality of human wholeness, it is a basic component. While physical healing is not the same as personal healing, it is intrinsically related. And while creative medicine will not usher in the kingdom of God, it can contribute significantly to that fuller realization of our common humanity, which is both a gift and an achievement.

James B. Nelson [1]

Some of the most perplexing moral problems to be faced today are in the field of biomedical ethics. Not only are these biomedical issues complex but they are matters that touch the lives of every one of us at some time or another. These issues deserve our careful attention, creative thinking, and concentrated energy.

One of the "good news—bad news" stories making the rounds concerns an airline pilot who addressed his passengers as follows: "Good afternoon, ladies and gentlemen. This is your pilot speaking. We are flying at an altitude of thirty-five thousand feet and a speed of seven hundred miles per hour. I have two pieces of news to report, one good and one bad. The bad news is that we are lost. The good news is that we are making very good time."

Some say that this announcement describes precisely the situation related to biomedical ethics. They say that we are already lost, and yet we are still moving very fast. This book has been prepared in the belief that our biomedical future is not predetermined. It is easy to get lost in a maze of biomedical issues. Events are developing almost too rapidly to keep up with. But the situation is not hopeless. There are resources in the Christian community to help us deal with these biomedical issues.

Against the contemporary backdrop of concern about biomedical ethics, this book has been written to provide Christian insights. The purpose of the book is threefold. In the first place, it has been put together in the belief that Christianity is a religion that speaks to all issues of life. Nothing is outside the scope of Christian truth. All truth is Christ's truth. Biomedical issues require information and insights from many disciplines. But we can begin by saying that Christianity provides both wisdom and motivation to deal with these biomedical issues.

Some say that Christianity has nothing to do with biomedical issues. They argue that these are medical, biological, and genetic problems. Such a view of life is too narrow, too provincial, too isolated from the wholeness of reality. It fails to take into account the need of an interdisciplinary approach to these issues. Such a view fails to understand that not everything that is scientifically possible is morally responsible.

On the other hand, there are those who say that theology provides all we need to deal with biomedical issues. These people cite a Scripture text and rush off, leaving the doctor, the biologist, the nurse, and the geneticist to struggle with these problems. Such a view is actually a violation of the biblical insight that we are to work with God in caring for creation. We are called to use all possible resources to find solutions to these problems. Jesus taught that his disciples are salt and light, penetrating the world to do God's good will (Matt. 5:13–16).

One purpose of the book, therefore, is to bring together insights from Christianity and the sciences. It is our intention to relate Christian ethics to crucial issues for which there are no easy answers. The matters discussed are controversial. There will be differences of opinion. But remember that underlying all the ideas presented is a unity based on the revelation of God in Jesus Christ.

The second purpose is to identify some of the perplexing problems related to biomedical ethics. We will seek to raise the right questions about some of the crucial issues of life. There are many matters which clamor for our attention in society, but the issue of biomedical ethics deserves special attention at this time. Let's face it! The church needs to give more attention to biomedical ethics. We have neglected these issues. They are tough. They are complex. They are usually gray instead of black and white. There are few precedents for some of the decisions that have to be made. So this book has been put together to try to ask the right questions and identify the right issues which must be faced.

What kind of issues are we talking about when we focus on biomedical ethics? Here are some examples of biomedical decisions that people in our society must face:

How should society determine who gets dialysis machines when there are not enough for all who need them?

Should prospective parents "make arrangements" to determine the sex, height, and perhaps IQ of their children before conception?

Should genetic screening be applied to everybody before marriage and childbearing to prevent defective or disease-prone babies from being conceived?

What about the morality of the practice of producing babies through test-tube union of sperm and egg?

Who should decide if and when a life-sustaining respirator is to be turned off?

Who should decide when an abortion is to take place?

Should imprisoned criminals be made docile through the use of drugs?

How should we determine when a person is legally dead?

Should society allow the practice of cloning if this process of producing a whole organism from a single cell is ever perfected?

Should the transplant of embryos from one mother to another be permitted?

Here is another example of a biomedical issue to be faced. How shall we evaluate the "Living Will" which so many people are now signing? Here is a version of the will.

To my Family, my Physician, my Lawyer, my Clergyman, to any Medical Facility in whose care I happen to be and to any individual who may become responsible for my health, welfare or affairs:

If the time comes when I can no longer take part in decisions for my own future, let this statement stand as an expression of my wishes, while I am still of sound mind.

If the situation should arise in which there is no reasonable expectation of my recovery from physical or mental disability, I request that I be allowed to die and not be kept alive by artificial means or "heroic measures." I do not fear death itself as much as the indignities of deterioration, dependence and hopeless pain. I, therefore, ask that medication be mercifully administered to me to alleviate suffering even though this may hasten the moment of death.

This living will is made after careful consideration. I hope you who care for me will feel bound to follow its mandate. I recognize that this appears to place a heavy responsibility upon you, but it is with the intention of relieving you of such responsibility and of placing it upon myself in accordance with my strong convictions, that this statement is made.

Signed _____

Date _____[2]

Issues such as these must be studied and evaluated by the Christian community. This book will spotlight some of these issues and provide resources for deciding what is right or wrong.

A final purpose of this study is to bear witness to the fact that the church can get involved in helping people find solutions to these problems. The church must provide resources to help the overworked nurse care for a dying patient; to help the troubled geneticist who struggles with the complexities of genetic screening; to help doctors who are trying to decide which patients to select for chronic dialysis treatment; to help biologists who wonder where their experiments will take them and the human race; to help ministers deal with the ambiguity and complexity involved in counseling people who must make decisions about biomedical issues.

Through the church, therefore, people can be helped to make moral decisions about biomedical issues. This brings us to ask what task the Christian ethicist is to perform in helping people decide about these matters. Professor Harmon Smith states in his book entitled *Ethics and the New Medicine* that he understands "the contribution of the professional theological ethicist . . . largely in terms of assessing and reflecting critically upon the human values at stake in medical decisions within the context of our shared *de facto* Judeo-Christian heritage."[3]

It is not the task of the ethicist to provide all the answers but, according to Smith, "To help clarify and focus appropriate issues and problems and, in the measure to which it is fitting and desired, to participate in the adjudication of alternative choices and actions."[4] Furthermore, the ethicist may be called on to participate in determining which courses of action to take. This book seeks to lay a foundation for making some of these choices.

In the context of the church, people can be assisted in working out their own method of decision making which will enable them to make decisions themselves about complex biomedical issues.

When you have finished the pages of this book, you will not have all the answers to biomedical questions. But, hopefully, you will be motivated by what you read to get involved in actions to deal responsibly with these issues. And, hopefully, you will have received guidance in developing your own method of moral decision making about biomedical issues.

Having looked at the purposes of this study, our attention will turn first to the sources of ethical insights and then to an examination of the relevance of Christianity for dealing with biomedical issues.

Some Sources of Ethical Insights

What are the sources of insight that will help us make decisions about ethical issues related to biomedical issues? This question has been addressed in a creative way by Dr. Kenneth Vaux who is professor of Ethics and Theology at the Institute of Religion in Houston, Texas. In his book, *Biomedical Ethics: Morality for the New Medicine,* Vaux carefully explores the sources of ethical insights for dealing with biomedical issues.[5]

The first source of ethical insight discussed by Vaux is *retrospec-*

tive insight. This is insight from the past, from history, from memory. Here the resources of history, philosophy, and religion are brought into the decision making process.[6]

The second source of ethical insight is *introspective insight,* which comes from within, from the depths of being, from the present. Vaux places both conscience and common sense here.[7]

A third source of ethical insight is what Vaux terms *prospective insight.* Here he looks to the future, to that which is ahead. There are two ways that the future provides insights about ethical decisions. As human beings hope to become something, their hope actually shapes their future. The future also provides insights as we ponder the consequences of our behavior. Technology enables us to predict the consequences of certain biomedical decisions.[8]

What Vaux and other thinkers in the field of biomedical ethics are saying is that we must seek information from a wide variety of sources lest we take too provincial a view and miss information essential to responsible decisions. One area of relevant information is theology and it is to this field that we now turn.

The Relevance of Theology for Biomedical Issues

The contributions that Christian theology can make to the consideration of biomedical issues are substantial. It is not my purpose to develop the details of a theological approach here, but an outline of some relevant biblical principles will be sketched. Throughout you will find a variety of biblical principles applied to specific problems.

The Bible records the history of God's actions in our midst. It teaches that God is active in the world and he calls us to respond to what he is doing.[9] God is not a remote disinterested being. He is a down-to-earth God who cares about us and becomes involved with us.

God acts in the world as Creator, and this means there is order and purpose in the world he has made. The life he created is good and should be affirmed by us. The efforts of the sciences to find out the truth about all aspects of this world should be affirmed. After all, this is God's world. Any truth about it is God's truth!

We can respond to the Creator with gratitude and praise for what he has created. We can translate our gratitude into a daily appreciation for life. We can support the dignity and sacredness of human life and resist attempts to wantonly destroy or manipulate life. We can celebrate life in all its fullness and goodness. We can support those efforts in the biomedical fields to affirm and enhance the dignity of life.

A response to the Creator also involves the stewardship of life that has been given to us. We are called to respect our bodies. We are called to respect the bodies and the health of others. We are called by God to have dominion over nature (Gen. 1:28). Indeed we can respond to the Creator by joining with him to finish the work of creation. This dominion over nature, this work to finish creation is a God-given gift. It must not be solely a human endeavor.

The Bible also teaches that God acts in his world as Judge or Governor controlling what he has made, and condemning the misuse of creation. The gone-wrongness of our world contributes to the tough biomedical situations about which it is often so difficult to make decisions. The pride and self-centeredness that led to the fall of human beings also lead us to make choices that are contrary to God's intention. The horrors of Auschwitz should remind us of the harm that human beings—even "well-educated" human beings—are able to inflict on one another.

We are called, therefore, to respond to the Judge with repentance for our sins in this area of moral behavior. We are called to exercise discipline in biomedical actions. Discipline is needed to prevent that tampering with life which can bring destruction to the very nature of life. Discipline is needed by those engaged in DNA research which could lead to great advances for humanity or to the catastrophe that would come if dangerous genetic agents are created.

We must respond to the Judge therefore with the restraint of evil in society. Those concerned about the quality of life in society have the responsibility and the duty to restrain any evil whereby life is cheapened, abused, or wantonly destroyed.

God's activity in the world as Redeemer makes salvation possible. In Jesus Christ we have a model for the expression of love in all relationships. Indeed, Jesus gives us not only the model of love but the power to love. He teaches us how to forgive and he points the way to hope through participation in the community of faith.

Jesus shows us how to care for people. He commanded his disciples to "heal the sick" (Matt. 10:8). The example of Jesus in caring for the poor, the captives, the blind, the oppressed (Luke 4:18) shows us the way to help others. The actual healing of many by Jesus motivates us to follow in his footsteps by helping and healing others. His example prods us to search for new technologies, and new methods for helping others.

We can respond to the Redeemer with love. In the realm of biomedical issues and in all moral matters, this means letting love guide our decisions. In our relations with others, God's love as revealed in Jesus Christ must prevail. For example, one of the most serious problems related to human health is malnourishment. Love requires that we find ways to feed the hungry, and as we do so we will be dealing with a problem that leads to much sickness, suffering, and untimely death.

A response to God the Redeemer also means that we accept Christ's forgiveness of ourselves and share the good news of this forgiveness with others. As we get involved in biomedical issues we encounter many who need this word of forgiveness: the worried woman who feels guilt over an abortion; the researcher whose experiments have led to birth defects; the physician who feels that he has neglected a patient; the biologist whose brilliant discoveries have been misused by people intent on "germ" warfare. These people need the good news of forgiveness and so do we.

We can respond to the Redeemer by pointing to the hope in Christ which means there is an existence beyond this life which gives meaning to it and keeps us from making the present earthly life our ultimate concern. Stewardship requires that we seek ways to enhance human life. Our salvation lies not in turning people into superhuman beings. Salvation lies in a relationship to God in Jesus Christ, a relationship that will span all eternity.

The Swiss doctor Paul Tournier speaks to this hope in Christ as it relates to biomedical issues:

The whole of our inquiry into the meaning of medicine leads us to this: we are collaborators with God. He uses us to postpone death, prolonging life in order to procure that merciful respite of which we have spoken. The sole purpose of our labor is to give our patients a supreme opportunity of encountering Jesus Christ, and of binding themselves even more closely to him through faith.[10]

A response to the Redeemer means that we can join with others in the church, the community of hope, to struggle together with the incredibly complex biomedical issues which must be faced. It is through the community of the church that we can seek a broader wisdom. The interdisciplinary approach provided by the church can prevent the isolation which sometimes leads to selfish actions contrary to what is best for society.

In summary, we are called to respond to God as he acts in our midst. We can respond to God the Creator with gratitude, celebration, and stewardship. We are called to respond to God who is active as Judge with repentance, discipline, and restraint of evil in society. We respond to God who is active as Redeemer with love, with acceptance of forgiveness, and by participation in the community of hope.

These biblical principles have been sketched here to underscore the belief that theology is relevant to biomedical issues. Throughout the pages that follow the writers will show how theology relates to the matters which they will discuss. Throughout all these discussions we will look to Christ who gave us a model to follow in our attempts to help people face biomedical issues when he said: "I came that they may have life, and have it abundantly" (John 10:10).

Notes

[1] James B. Nelson, *Human Medicine* (Minneapolis: Augsburg Publishing House, 1973), p. 189.

[2] Prepared by Euthanasia Educational Council—Nashville Chapter.

[3] Harmon L. Smith, *Ethics and the New Medicine* (Nashville: Abingdon Press, 1970), p. 13.

[4] Ibid.

[5] Kenneth Vaux, *Biomedical Ethics: Morality for the New Medicine* (New York: Harper & Row, 1974), pp. 37ff.

[6] Ibid., p. 30.

[7] Ibid., pp. 38–39.

[8] Ibid., pp. 44–45.

[9] This theme has been explored by H. Richard Niehbur in his classroom lectures and in his book, *The Responsible Self;* and it has been developed by E. Clinton Gardner in *Biblical Faith and Social Ethics* and by Waldo Beach in *The Christian Life.* The compiler of this book has applied this approach to sexuality in his book entitled *Thank God for Sex!*

[10] Paul Tournier, *A Doctor's Casebook in the Light of the Bible* (New York: Harper & Row, 1960), pp. 234–235.

2

The Christian Faith Speaks To The Questions Of Modern Medicine

Daniel B. McGee

Daniel B. McGee asks extremely important questions related to biomedical issues: (1) Should we play God? (2) What guidelines should we follow? (3) How do we define human life? (4) Who should decide? (5) What should we do first?

The answers that Dr. McGee gives to these pivotal questions grow out of his deep belief that we are to participate with God in his work in all areas of life including biomedical issues. A central thrust of the chapter is the need for dialogue between people in various fields of science and religion. Decisions about biomedical issues must grow out of this dialogue through a communal process.

Since 1966, Dr. McGee has served as a professor in the Department of Religion at Baylor University, Waco, Texas. He is a pioneer among Southern Baptists in the area of biomedical issues. He is active in church and community affairs, and has written numerous articles on medical ethics, environmental ethics, economic ethics, and political ethics.

His interpretations of biomedical issues from the perspective of Christian theology have helped shape the thinking of many young people and adults throughout the country.

The Christian Faith Speaks To The Questions Of Modern Medicine

Astonishment, fear, gratitude, questions—these are the consequences of advances in medical technology and practice. From the control of human reproduction to the management of the dying process, we have watched familiar landscapes being radically altered. Abortion, genetic modification, gender selection, behavior modification, cloning, organ transplants, artificial insemination, prolongation of life—these are examples of the practices that have alternately created optimistic astonishment and fearful anxiety in the soul of contemporary humanity. These hopes and fears are reflected in large measure by the recurring questions growing out of these practices. Should we play God? What guidelines should we follow? How do we define human life? Who should decide? What should we do first? These are the questions I want us to examine, and to reflect on the answers suggested by the Christian faith.

Should We Play God?

The tragic experience with the Philadelphia Legionnaires is only one of many reminders that we are not gods. We are not all-knowing. We are not omnipotent. We are not morally perfect. Like all humankind of all generations past, present, or future, we see through a glass darkly. Even our best efforts are marred by our own corruption, our own weakness, and our own ignorance.

Does this mean that we fold our tents and steal away to a quiet land of passive contemplation? Do we fold our hands in the belief that it is all in God's hands—or nature's hands—or in the hands of an all-powerful technological advance?

The Christian faith affirms that humankind's role in the making of history is not that of a spectator. We are called by God to be participants in the making of history—co-workers with God to accomplish that good which God wills and works toward.

In medicine we have been cursed by a religious view called "God of the Gaps Theology." This view holds that all areas of life beyond human understanding or control comprise God's territory—a turf from which humankind is forever banned. From this perspective it appears that every new human venture is an assault upon the Godhead, a usurpation of God's prerogatives. Thus we hear such appealing but inaccurate cries as: "Only God decides when a person dies." "Only God creates life." The truth is that from the very beginning God has called us to be co-creators and co-preservers of human life. The difference today, and it is a dramatic difference, is that our capacity for controlling life has greatly increased. How do we respond?

In Christ, God confronted mankind with new challenges and new demands. That same Christ told those who listened to him to stop burying their talents and to invest them. He also told them to stop putting their light under a bushel, to expose it. He told them to leave the settled ways of their homes and work and to follow him into new lands and new tasks. When John the Baptist inquired about this new ministry Christ replied: "Go and tell John what you have seen and heard: the blind receive their sight, the lame walk, lepers are cleansed, and the deaf hear, the dead are raised up, the poor have good news preached to them. And blessed is he who takes no offense in me" (Luke 7:22–23, RSV). Christ invited those who followed to take no offense in his healing but to join him in that ministry. We have the same invitation today.

Christ calls us to be faithful stewards using responsibly that which we have been entrusted. We are today a generation remarkably endowed with capacities and opportunities only dreamed of in the past. The typical image of the country doctor was of one stepping back from the bed and saying, "Well, it's in God's hands now." We are God's stewards and have been given the frightening and exhilarating responsibility of managing the benefits the master of the household intends for his family. We have been entrusted with the miracles of modern medicine.

There are two ways a steward can fail. One is to avoid the responsibility. The other is to misuse it. We turn to the latter possibility with our next question.

What Guidelines Should We Follow?

If we are to be participants and not spectators in the arena of history, then we must consider the rules or guidelines by which we are to participate. The steward can be faithless by diverting the master's resources to goals and purposes other than the master's. The biblical tradition describes this as the sinful tendency of those who have been blessed. In Deuteronomy, chapters 8 and 9, are found two false explanations by God's elect for why it is they are so fortunate to possess the promised land. First, they claim that it is by their own might that the possession of the land has occurred. They are self-made men constantly astonished at their own brilliance and achievements. The second explanation attributes their possessions to their own righteousness. Their moral superiority has earned for them their good fortune. Those explanations are rejected by a biblical faith in its claim that all good gifts come from God.

In the heady excitement of the truly miraculous achievements in medical technology, we are tempted to explain it all by self-indulgent praise of our own brilliance or goodness. We then use these claims to create the myth that we are our own master, owing nothing to anyone, and, therefore, free to do with our capacities and resources whatever we will. On occasions we might create new gods in our own image and then serve them. Some have done this with science or technology, willing to let them take their own course. Thus if it can be done, it should be done. The Christian faith points to a different explanation and a different behavior. The God revealed in Christ is the master—not ourselves—not our science—not our medical technology. Therefore we are responsible to make this technology serve the will of God.

In describing God's will we describe the purpose we are to make our medicine serve. In the biblical tradition God's will is defined in terms of God's action. God's will is not hidden from us but is revealed in the acts of God as witnessed to in the Judeo-Christian tradition. While the acts of God are rich in their diversity and often disputed in their interpretations, we must and can sketch the major features of God's will to serve as guidelines for our behavior.

The profile of God's activity that comes through to me most clearly is of a God who is obsessed with giving life and life more abundantly to humankind. I see a God who in creation is pictured as working to create a life, a community, and an environment that would provide the richest and most rewarding experience possible for his children. This is the same God who in Christ showed himself by serving whatever human needs he encountered. I see a God who says to his stewards, "Make medicine serve human needs and nothing else." The temptation is for technology to serve itself—for medical institutions to serve themselves—for medical professionals to serve their professional advancement—for research to serve research—for social, medical, and religious customs to serve themselves. When this happens we must be jerked back to the vision of a Christ who when challenged for healing on the sabbath said: "The sabbath was made for man and not man for the sabbath." Medicine, hospitals, research, medical procedures, and moral guidelines are made for man. They, like the sabbath, are gifts from God to serve humanity. Human life was not created to serve them.

How Do We Define Human Life?

If we are to serve human life, what are the qualities to be served? The attempt to define human life is ancient. The success of such attempts is questionable. However, even after recognizing both the difficulty and the danger, it is important for Christians to examine their tradition for insights as to what qualities or features of human life are to be served.

First of all, our bodies, our biological activity is a genuine part of our humanity. The creation story in Genesis 2 pictures God as creating a body, breathing into it life, and the total result is a soul. The notion of a radical dualism between the body and spirit is a Greek idea, alien to biblical tradition. The early Christian ministers response to the doctrine of the bodily resurrection reflects this perception that a part of our real self (humanity) is our body.

This means that if I love you I must concern myself with what we have unfortunately categorized as your physical needs. The ministry to the medical needs of God's children needs to be as crucial a concern for the church as it was for Christ.

Also, if our humanity is bodily, then we are limited in terms of time, space, and power. We never pretend that we have unlimited capacities. Nor should we curse our limitations and dream of some technological Eden when we will overcome our limitations. They are a part of who we are.

Finally we should respect the biological order and system that is a part of who we are. This is not a call for "letting nature take its course" as we will see in a moment. However, those who treat, for example, our genetic tradition as if it were void of purpose, needing to be radically reordered, fail to appreciate what has been given in our biological heritage.

Is that all that can be said about how God has created us? Of course not. If it were, the distinction between humankind and the animal kingdom would be slight.

God has created us with a freedom and individuality that comprises an essential part of our humanity. God created man in his own image. That is, God created us with a will of our own that gives us the awesome capacity to participate meaningfully in shaping our lives and our futures. Thus, if I love you, I will respect your freedom to be you. I will acknowledge that you are different from me and I will defend your right to retain that difference.

I am concerned about many of the proposals in genetic and behavior modification that fail to value the diversity of humanity. They would eliminate all the "weirdos." What concerns me is that from someone's perspective each of us is weird. Diversity and individuality is essential to our humanity. I do not mean there is no place for modification. What concerns me are the purposes to which some would direct it. Great care must be taken to preserve our freedom and diversity because that is how God created us.

We should also remember this as we consider the purposes and the results of medical experimentation, gender determination, cloning, and the prolongation of life. We must always consider human freedom if we are to emulate the creative God who gave that freedom to all of us as a distinctive part of our humanity.

God created us not only in freedom but also in community. To be human is to be in community with others. Again, the creation stories of Genesis 1 and 2 instruct us. In chapter 2, God's creation is not complete with one Adam. There must be two, in community complementing and fulfilling each other. The entire biblical story can be read as God's attempt to reconcile the brokenness of humanity and return us to his original intent—an unbroken community in which the individuals complete each other's humanity. To be human is to be social. Contrary to popular belief, our individuality and our sociality are not contradictory. You must have both or you have neither. The only way to have community is to begin with unique individuals. The only way unique individuals can realize their full humanity is to have others complement them (see 1 Cor. 12:4–26).

Who Should Decide?

The implications of our communal nature are many but one of the most important is in answering the question, "Who should decide?" Who decides if and when to pull the plug? Who decides if and when to abort? Who decides if and when and in what way to modify behavior? Who decides which patient receives the scarce organ for transplantation? Who decides? The physician? The patient? The family? The insurance company? The preacher? The hospital administrator? The legislator?

While the immediate locus of decision making may shift from one situation to another, the crucial truth is that our decision making must be communal. There is no place for Lone Rangers. No single person and no single group has the wisdom to assume the role of the decision maker. As we have become more specialized vocationally, we have become less informed generally and thus more dependent upon others. We must then be driven to the kind of cooperative effort described in 1 Corinthians 12:4–26. Here, no one organ can pretend to be the whole body. In medicine the issues are too complex and too important to be left to physicians to decide by themselves. Indeed most of them recognize this. There are factors (such as social factors) that escape the view of the physician where attention is concentrated upon the medical information.

Certainly no one removed from the medical scene, such as a theologian, can provide definitive decisions. Each of us alone is inadequate to decide. Thus we must develop procedures that deliberately secure input from as many sources of insight as possible. This includes all those mentioned above plus such people as social workers, economists, lawyers, and all members of the health care team. This process requires compromising, a dirty word to some. Without a cooperative give-and-take there can be no human community. The camel may be a horse created by a committee but I will take that compromised camel any day over the stubborn donkey who insists that the whole world yield to his idiosyncrasy.

There is a special problem for Christians in a pluralistic society where communal decisions must be made. We cannot assume that the state exists to enforce the moral conscience of the church upon all society. You and I must make a clear distinction between that behavior we as Christians would defend and that behavior we would force upon everyone. This distinction is crucial if we are to maintain the proper church-state relationship. It is especially relevant when considering the abortion issue.

What Should We Do First?

With the plethora of issues and responsibilities that confront us in bio-ethics, where do we begin? The truth is that we have to begin everywhere at once. None of the responsibilities can be avoided. However, there can be some priorities. One of our responsibilities is to determine which needs receive priority attention. We tend to follow the headlines—the dramatic—the unusual—the esoteric—the futuristic. It may be that the greatest need lies elsewhere. The common, and therefore, forgotten need demands attention. The truth is that the greatest health hazard in the world today is inadequate food. Not organ transplants, not chemotherapy, not psychosurgery, but food is the health need that touches most of the human race today. In deciding what we do first it is important to remember that as we debate genetic modification to increase the IQ of future generations, many of the present generation's children are being retarded by insufficient protein in their diets. Of course, there is a reason to fix our attention upon the unusual and the futuristic. We don't have to do much about them but talk. The immediate and the common demand action now. Christ showed us the way. He went to the hospital ward at the pool of Bethzatha and healed first the one who had been most overlooked, the one who had waited the longest and who had no friend.

The issue most in need of attention today is health care delivery. There are large segments of the world's population (many within our own society) whose medical services are at a primitive stage. That is where we begin. Just distribution of the resources we have is the first task. While we debate the future we must achieve justice in the present. While we consider the novel, we must not overlook the common needs.

What is the future of our medicine? It depends on how we answer the questions. Shall we play god? No, but we have no excuse in avoiding the responsibility of being God's co-worker in the task of managing our medical resources. What shall be our guidelines? The acts of God show us the way. There we see a God whose obsession is to serve human need. How do we define human life? God has created us bodily and with a freedom and individual uniqueness that requires special protection. Furthermore, we have been created as communal beings. Therefore, we advance the quality of human existence wherever we promote reconciliation or the capacity of one human being to have fellowship with another. Who shall decide? The decisions are so important and so complex that only our communal wisdom will be adequate. In finding ways to decide together we become more like the community of humanity which God created us to be. What do we do first? Justice in health care delivery is the immediate task. While we tease our minds with th unique dilemmas of modern medicine we must not overlook a. ancient problem—the weak, the forgotten, the unpopular are not getting to the healing waters. Only as we see and follow the example of Christ will we hear, "Well done, good and faithful servant; you have been faithful over a little, I will set you over much; enter into the joy of your master" (Matt. 25:21, RSV).

3
Bioethical Issues
In Behavior Control
Wayne E. Oates

A basic primer on behavior control is offered in this chapter by
Dr. Wayne E. Oates. After surveying some of the technologies of
behavior control, attention is given to some ethical issues that relate
to the freedom and dignity of human life.

These words of Dr. Oates flow from his strong belief that biomedical issues must be related to our knowledge of God as revealed to us
in Jesus Christ. The fact that Dr. Oates has served as a teacher in a
theological seminary and in a university medical school is a demon-
stration of his methodology of seeking to discover and act on the
basis of the best insights of religion and the sciences.

Dr. Oates presently serves as professor of Psychiatry and Behavioral Sciences at the University of Louisville School of Medicine.
He is also director, Program in Ethics and Pastoral Counseling at
the University of Louisville School of Medicine. From 1948 to 1974,
Dr. Oates was professor of Psychology of Religion at Southern
Baptist Theological Seminary in Louisville. A prolific and profound
writer, Dr. Oates has authored many books in his field. He is one of
the outstanding people in the field of psychology and religion
throughout the world.

Bioethical Issues
In Behavior Control

Immanuel Kant said that "the universal law of right may be expressed thus: 'Act externally in such a manner that the free exercise of your will may be able to coexist with the freedom of all others, according to a universal law.' Ethics imposes upon me the obligation to make the fulfillment of right a *maxim* of my conduct."[1] The application of "the universal law of right" to the differential diagnoses of biomedical decision making involves a molecular, interacting field of persons. Their freedom has to coexist with each other in order that right may be exercised. The purposes of this chapter are as follows: (1) To identify the specific tools of behavior control now in use in the fields of psychology and psychiatry, (2) to clarify and state some major ethical issues involved in the use of these tools insofar as the inherent ambiguity of human life will permit, (3) to relate these tools and issues to our knowledge of God as we have been enabled to know God in Jesus Christ.

What Is Behavior Control?

Behavior control refers to the personal or technological power to intervene in the functions of another person. The emotional functions of the other person, the behavioral patterns of another person, and even the belief patterns of another person are interfered with in such ways as to cause that person to conform to the prechosen emotions, behaviors, and beliefs of the person or persons doing the intervening. In short, behavior control refers to the use of psychological and/or psychiatric technology to alter the thought and behavior of individuals.[2] Earlier the issues concerning behavior control, concerned with the involuntary and indeterminate commitment of mentally ill patients, were the focus of the issues of human rights. This concern still exists. More recently, a new climate of concern has arisen over the powers of psychologists and psychiatrists (to say nothing of the media and advertisement industries) to shape behavior. However, we grope with the fear that technologists of behavior control will exercise their will freely without regard to the freedom of persons whom they treat. Thus patients will be subtly or forthrightly deprived of their human freedom.

The Technologies of Behavior Control

The specific technologies of behavior control can be identified and described as follows:

Milieu Therapy

Milieu therapy is the scientific programming of the environment of the hospital situation. The objective is to change the personality of the patient. Schedules of activities such as picnics, buffet suppers, dances, and card games, et cetera, are arrayed around other treatment modalities such as drug therapy, shock therapy, and individual psychotherapy. Critical issues arise in this kind of therapy. It can become an unreal environment so different from the demands of the patient's workaday world that the patient is prone to stay in treatment indefinitely. The contemporary support of patients with insurance aids and abets this by taking the edge off the financial motive for getting back into the nonhospital world. The ethical issue of the weight of the cost of this kind of treatment on the rest of the family is a second issue. Milieu treatment can be a means for doctors paying less personal attention to the patient. Staff indecision about the treatment plans while physicians spend considerable amounts of time in private psychotherapy with nonhospitalized patients is probably the most critical issue. As one patient put it, "I spend all of my week with people who are least responsible for and equipped to treat me. I rarely get to see the person who makes the decision as to whether I am to be kept in the hospital or discharged."

Individual Psychotherapy

The individual psychotherapist depends upon the conversational relationship between the patient and himself. He employs devices and strategies which meet the person at his own level "for the explicit intent of reaching mutual understanding through the process of insightful learning. The therapist may, at times, focus on removing symptoms, but not as an end in itself. He may employ ventilation, reeducation, clarification, interpretation, modeling, and many other modalities for the purpose of alleviating an undue degree of suffering, such as, feelings of alienation, rejection, sadness, guilt, aggression and sexual unrest."[3]

The critical issues involved in individual psychotherapy are the length of the treatment process, the emotional exploitation of the client for sexual or power purposes, the expense for the treatment in terms of the actual removal of the symptoms which bring the patient into treatment, and the way in which the more or less rational approaches to the problems may substitute talk for action. The heavy criticisms of these issues have been most responsibly stated by William Glasser in his book, *Reality Therapy.*[4]

Group Psychotherapy

The central hypothesis of group psychotherapy is that the isolation, brokenness, and behavioral deviance of a given individual have sprung from his/her relationship to significant groups. Therefore, if the person's behavior and values are to be changed, the group itself is the medium of control. Leadership style has much to do with the ethical quality of the group life. A leader may range all the way from a dictatorial personality upon whom the group members depend and by whom they are subjected to forced indoctrination to a completely laissez-faire leader who insists that all issues be dealt with and resolved by the group. Critical issues arise (1) as to the relationship of the group to other groups and to the larger milieu, (2) as to the right of a member of the group to discuss matters with persons whose lives are affected who are not members of the group, such as a spouse or a parent, (3) as to the degree to which the use of groups becomes an easy answer to the shortage of personnel in the institution where group therapy is the method of choice. Probably, however, the most critical issue is whether the leader is a competent and experienced person, which is the criterion of selecting group leaders.

Drug Therapy

Probably the most widely used technology for behavior control today is psychotropic drugs. The galaxy of different drugs is overwhelming to the lay person. A classification of drugs and their uses in behavior control can be briefly presented here.

Maintenance control drugs are used in rather commonly known instances. For example, in epilepsy dilantin and phenobarbital are used on a regular, maintenance basis. In diabetes, insulin is a maintenance medication of choice. In withdrawn, senile persons, as well as hyperkinetic children, Ritalin (Methylphenidate hydrochloride) is used. Minor tranquilizers such as Librium (Chlordiazepoxide) or Valium (Diazepam) are used in controlling muscle spasms, controlling hysteria in acute grief reactions, and in enabling highly compulsive people to work more effectively.

Antidepressants. Mood changing drugs are administered on several hypotheses, one of which is that catecholamines (epinephrine, noreprenephrine, and dopamine) are deficient in supply and therefore disrelate the neurotransmitters to each other causing depression. The introduction of such drugs as Tofranil (imipramine), Elavil (amitriptyline), and other closely related compounds, allowed physicians to estimate that 32 to 80 percent improvement occurs depending upon the criterion for diagnosis and improvement.

A longer term, more nearly maintenance kind of medication for persons suffering from bipolar or manic-depressive illness is lithium carbonate. I have seen at least two patients hitherto nonfunctional able to work and be remarkably creative as long as they "stayed on" lithium. The chemical formula and hypotheses of this medication are different from the MAO inhibitors.

Phenothiazine derivatives, over two dozen in number, are used to treat schizophrenic disorders, reducing thought disorders, loss of self-care motivation, and paranoid symptoms. The "workhorse" medication is chlorpromazine (Thorazine). As in the case of lithium as a long-term maintenance drug, prolixim has similar effects for schizophrenics. The present issue of treatment seems to revolve around the low-dosage-high-dosage concepts. Some of those who have the facilities to keep a patient in longer term psychotherapy and to maintain extensive milieu therapy tend to rely upon low-dosage approaches. Some of those who have limited facilities and less affluent patients tend to move toward high dosage treatment. In fact some studies indicate that as one moves higher up the social ladder, the treatment of choice tends to rely less and less upon medication therapy and more upon milieu therapy and psychotherapy.[5] One critical ethical issue rests at the point of the ways in which more rapid and intensive forms of therapy are provided for the poor against the more leisure expensive forms of treatment for the affluent. To what extent do private hospitals *need* the affluent patient more than the patient needs them?

Aversion Therapy

Aversion therapy is the attempt to change and/or control undesirable behavior by presenting an exceptionally unpleasant stimulation in conjunction with or as a result of the behavior. For example antabuse is an aversive treatment for alcoholism. If the person is on antabuse, and if that person ingests alcohol, then the person becomes nauseated, vomits, has throbbing headaches, has a fall in blood pressure, and develops labored breathing and blurred vision. Sexual deviants may be treated in another aversive form of therapy. Pornographic pictures may be presented and an electric impulse presented at the same time as a shock device. The temporary results of such treatment are the most outstanding characteristic, in my opinion.

Electroconvulsive Therapy

Electroconvulsive therapy, commonly known as "shock therapy" has been in use since the early 1940s. Originally thought to be a counteragent for schizophrenic behavior, it is now largely focused

on the treatment of depressive patients. Hamilton and others place
ECT above drug therapy for depression, but considerable numbers
of clinicians feel that drug therapy is the treatment of choice. I work
in two psychiatric facilities. In Louisville General Hospital, shock
therapy is not used at all. In the Norton Psychiatric Clinic, a private
hospital, it is used only occasionally. In the early years of the use of
ECT, it was almost a panacea, because little else was available at the
somatic level of treatment except custodial care and such things as
hydrotherapy. Rather than being a panacea, it was probably a form
of desperation.

Psychosurgery

With the advent of the psychotropic drugs, psychosurgery went
into a decline. We are experiencing a resurgence of the art now
because of the refining of the procedures, the claimed successes
with the drug addicts, homosexuals, patients with intolerable pain,
severe obsessional neurotic behavior, and other conditions. The
common feature of all psychosurgical inventions is reduction of
response to unpleasant stimuli. It does not remove the symptoms
but reduces the responses to the symptoms. A patient hearing
voices may continue to do so, but pays less attention to them.[6]
Psychosurgery is done, not by psychiatrists, but by neurosurgeons.
The psychiatrists select the patients, however. It is a *last* treatment,
after all other methods have been used. Therefore, it is impossible
to compare and contrast it effectively with other forms of treatment.

Electronic Stimulation of the Brain

A technique of behavior control has been developed in which tiny
electric drills are used to bore holes in the skull. Then electrical
conductors are placed at strategic locations in the brain with the
objective of inducing the thought, feeling, or behavior associated
with that section of the brain. A clinic has been established in
Boston to treat patients who have uncontrollable rage periods. The
important issue to consider here ethically is that the rage may be
evoked or terminated, as determined by the physician.

Stereotaxic psychosurgery is a form of treatment used at the fringes of psychiatric and psychological practice to control behavior. It consists of placing the patient's head in a firm and stable position, drilling a hole in the skull from a specific angle indicated by the knowledge of the neurosurgeon about the function and location of specific areas of the brain. A knife or an electrode may be used to accomplish the results intended. The most used and reliable results of this surgery have been with parkinsonism in operations on the thalamus of the patient. Dramatic relief of symptoms has been achieved. However, more recent uses of this kind of surgery have been aimed at the alteration of certain parts of the brain to control violent, aggressive behavior. Also, homosexuals have allegedly been turned straight by surgical changes in what is known as Cajal's nucleus in the brain, the section supposedly governing the sexual behavior of persons.

Two Japanese neurosurgeons initiated stereotaxic surgery in 1951. Their initial efforts were to devise surgical procedures to correct temporal lobe epilepsy. Then it was extended to include patients with combined electroencephalogram abnormalities and marked behavior disturbances. These doctors were Hirataro Narabayashi and Y. Uchimura. The cases cited by them were all accompanied by neurological pathology such as mental retardation, extreme lack of control of aggressive behavior, and post-encephalitic behavior. None of these cases were used to demonstrate that criminal or deviant behavior without concomitant neurological abnormalities were the targets of such surgery.[7] Valenstein in commenting upon such operations as a deterrent to aggressive behavior and/or undesirable sexual behavior says: "The changes that can follow . . . can be very unpredictable and far reaching. Characterizing the total effects of these operations by such phrases as 'taming' and 'hypersexuality' can be very misleading . . . different and opposite behavior changes can be expressed under other circumstances."[8]

Anectine Therapy

Anectine (Succynlcholine Chloride) is a powerful muscle relaxant used in anesthesia and as an adjunct to administering electroconvulsive therapy. Apparently a patient remains conscious throughout the time of the drug's effects, but the main effect is immobilized skeletal musculature. During the entire time the patient receives supplemental oxygen, he is conscious and can comprehend what is going on around him. The patient is "counseled while he is under the drug." This drug has been used in one experiment at least at the Vacaville, California facility for treating sociopathic offenders against the law as well as at a state hospital and a prison for women in California. They are persons who had attacked others, been extremely self-destructive, and were generally extremely angry persons. Under the influence of the drug they were counseled to realize how dangerous their behavior was to themselves and others and to learn to be as free of the impulse to violence as they were while under the influence of anectine. The anectine treatment is a combination of hypnosis, operant conditioning, classical conditioning, and even punitive treatment. It has been discontinued in California treatment facilities because it does not accomplish anything that forms of behavioral modification can accomplish without chemical intervention.

Behavior Modification

Most of the previously mentioned forms of behavior control have been the province of psychiatrists. The contribution of psychologists to behavior control has been through various forms of behavior modification and/or behavioral therapy. Such treatment modalities may be either of a classical conditioning variety or of an operant conditioning variety. Classical conditioning is "respondent" or Type S conditioning. In it a person responds positively or negatively to a given stimulus. When that stimulus is repeated, then the person responds similarly. "Extinguishing" an undesirable trait may consist of "flooding" the patient with stimuli such as a thing he may fear until the fear is extinguished; or, it may consist of intermittently presenting the patient with the stimulus.

The other kind of behavioral therapy is operant conditioning, which works on behavior that is strengthened or weakened by its consequences rather than its antecedents. B. F. Skinner refers to the Christian teachings concerning heaven and hell as subsequent consequences to behavior. "The power achieved by the religious agency depends upon how effectively certain verbal reinforcements are conditioned—in particular the promise of heaven and the threat of hell."[9]

In hospitals a "token economy" is developed in which persons are rewarded or deprived of things they want in proportion to the way they accomplish the simpler tasks of socialization, such as arising at a certain time, bathing themselves, attending and participating in certain activities, et cetera. Tokens or script can be used to buy things for themselves, to admit them to movies, et cetera.

Several therapeutic and ethical concerns have been raised by the American Psychiatric Association concerning behavioral therapy. (1) The inadequate and partial training of many persons doing the therapy is likely to reduce the therapy to techniques without broader understanding. (2) The lack of supervisors with clinical experience may cause the therapist to overlook or ignore personal relationships to the patient and fail to provide the patient with support, guidance, advice, encouragement, reassurance, and clarification. (3) The possibility that sociopolitical and ethnic behaviors will become the target of treatment as a latent form of social control or forced indoctrination. (4) The ethical problem of coercive manipulation is another form of the third threat. (5) The possibility that the programs will become nontherapeutic ways of punishing behavior and rationalizing sadistic behavior. These are legitimate ethical concerns. Any one of them could be true of psychiatric methods of therapy such as shock therapy, drug therapy or lobotomies. Any one of them can be applied to pastoral counseling, use of the Bible, prayer, and church participation. The hand and motive of the user shapes the efficacy of any form of treatment.[10]

Critical Issues of Human Rights

After such a labyrinthine survey of technologies of behavior control, we need to face the critical issues in human freedom and dignity involved in the use of these methods in controlling human behavior.

1. The Issue of Survival. Psychiatrists and psychologists and other specialists working in the treatment settings are concerned with minimal function for effective survival. B. F. Skinner defines values this way: "Things are good (positively reinforcing) or bad (negatively reinforcing) presumably because of the contingencies of survival under which the species evolved."[11] Survival is a powerful motive for behavior. A young person working in a Louisville Boatworks finds after two years that there must be some better way to make a living and decides to go to college. This is an everyday, normal example of what Skinner means. However, the clinician psychiatrist, psychologist, and clinically expert minister are concerned with such elemental survival as a person being willing to eat, as in the case of the mental patient who is starving himself to death (anorexia nervosa). We are interested in patients being able to tell what time of day it is, where they are, and what their names are. We are interested in their being clothed and in their right minds. We are interested in their being able to feed themselves, shelter themselves, and to pay for these things through having been gainfully employed.

The measures of behavior control that I have previously described here have these minimal goals in mind. The issues of values at this point of survival are minimal. However, when these technologies are applied to more complex values, such as the appropriate response to injustice, the nature of one's political behavior and one's religious beliefs, the peril increases. When a staff is concerned with whether the patient is going to kill himself or someone else if discharged, then the goals of behavior control are much more concrete, circumscribed, and desperate. Persons who have never struggled with these issues of survival with patients can afford the luxury of being abstract and debonair about the rights of persons. But the clinician needs to lift his head up from such problems long enough to ask some more philosophical and ethical questions.

A case in point: an upper middle-class woman comes to the emergency psychiatric center of a hospital. She is saturated internally with alcohol and permeates the air with the smell of it. She is medically on the verge of delirium tremens. She has no adult relatives in the city; only a daughter who is a minor. She has had an automobile accident in the last twelve hours with only property damage. She will not voluntarily be admitted to the hospital. The staff uses its legal authority to hold her for forty-eight hours against her will. She is placed in the acute room and given Valium intramuscularly to offset delirium tremens. She is prevented from killing herself or someone else or both in an auto accident until her adult relatives can come and take responsibility for her. We require her to act externally in such a manner that her exercise of her will will coexist with the freedom of others to live and do well, too.

However, if we were to use the power to control her life in such a way as to determine her political, religious, and economic beliefs, her capacity to use what autonomy of judgment she does have, then, as Philip Roos says, "the ethical question can be raised as to what degree and under what conditions is the shaping of social behavior to be sanctioned?"[12] Similarly, the use of religious sanctions outside a hospital setting to overcontrol the behavior of persons was questioned early by Freud. He accused families of having conditioned children to fit into the parent's programs when they were too young to defend themselves. Such could be exemplified in the provision of hamburgers and money given to children who are bused by churches who aspire to be the world's largest church. The same ethical conditions prevail.

Where we as Christians would challenge the behavior modification theorists is exactly at the point that they become theorists. The issue is *the selection of goals* for the conditioning. What are the goals and what was the due process in the selection of the goals? It is one thing to prevent a person from driving a car when on the verge of delirium tremens. It is another to administer Valium if she has objections on the grounds that she is a Christian Scientist. This is seen by Bruce J. Ennis, a lawyer, as an unnecessary concomitant of hospitalization.[13] Furthermore, we had to have data beyond a reasonable doubt that she was indeed dangerous to the lives of the children on her street. We had the eyewitness account of three neighbors as well as the account of her minor daughter.

What, therefore, are the goals of behavior control and who selects them? What are the values of those doing the selecting? In the name of scientific objectivity, some behavioral therapists will plead that they are neutral and have no values. One feels they protest too much. Charlotte Buhler, a therapist herself, says that "knowingly or unknowingly the therapist conveys something to the patient about values." Carrera and Adams say that "operant conditioning with children lends itself to the endorsement of what the parents want, without formal or ritualized appeal to any canons regarding the child's best interests." [14]

2. The Issue of the Patient's Best Interest. In the article by Carrera and Adams just quoted, a basic ethical issue is made of "the patient's best interests" in any kind of behavior control measure. In the Helsinki Declaration of the World Health Organization, special stress is laid upon the precariousness of the use of any means that weakens the physical or mental resistance of a person. They expect the physician to use only those means that are in "the best interest of the patient himself/herself." [15] In explaining this further, Seymour Halleck, M.D., insists that the patient's best interest consists in (1) *never* deceiving the patient, (2) taking care that overdiagnosis of dangerousness of the patient to himself and others is not done, (3) and of asking for a board of consultants in such cases as the prolonged use of tranquilizers, the use of irreversible procedures such as lobotomies, and the decision for long-term psychiatric hospitalization.

I personally would add that cases in which patients have been under treatment for more than six months be reviewed by a group of outside peers to see what the diagnosis is, what the treatment has been, and what the treatment plan is. Champus Insurance Company gives a foretaste of governmental monitoring of pastoral counseling and psychiatric treatment. The first eight interviews, a written diagnosis, plan of treatment, and prognosis is required. Beyond twenty interviews, a peer review organization report is required.

The iatronic disasters that occur in long-term psychiatric treatment become knowledge too often by accident and not plan. I myself have seen patients who have been in treatment for as many as twelve years, in one instance, and twenty-two in another. I am confident that the psychiatrist today has often become a sort of lifelong private chaplain of a secular nature to wealthy families. Much good has been done by these persons; however, descriptions of this treatment rarely appear in the literature. Nor is it held up to the light by day in answerability of one physician to his or her peers. The question one raises here ethically and practically is: "To what extent do such families need such care and to what extent does the psychiatrist need such patients?" Also, the same question could be raised about the pastoral care of such families.[16]

3. The Patient's Threat of Legal Action. The patients treated by psychologists and psychiatrists would not be candidates for such treatment if they were thoroughly rational persons. The dilemma arises when we insist that the ethical responsibility of the physician is to help the patient make a rational choice as to the desirability of the treatment. A reverse backlash has occurred at the clinical level of decision making about treatment as a result of the cancellation of malpractice insurance policies, the elevation of costs of such insurance, and so on.

Exceptional amounts of publicity have been given to professions who have a tradition of privacy—no advertisement for patients, and no public utterances that can be avoided. For example, a family member of a patient called me recently and asked that I see her daughter, a twenty-four-year-old woman. She said that she had seen five psychiatrists, and they all refused to treat her daughter. I asked her to tell me something of what she, the mother, felt was wrong with her daughter. She said that her daughter kept threatening suicide. I asked her if she felt her daughter needed around-the-clock attention to prevent this from happening. She said that she did and that she was worn out from doing so. I told her that I work as a professor in a department of psychiatry and that I would be legally culpable if I took her daughter as a counselee unless she was willing to go into a hospital.

The mother then said: "I don't think she ought to be in a hospital, and I refuse to see that happen." I then gently referred her to another pastoral counselor who is NOT a member of a department of psychiatry. The critical issue here is that of *defensive medicine*.

Physicians and those associated with them are refusing to take the risks involved in many treatment situations because *they* do not have the right to use their own judgment in treatment situations.

There is another side to this, however, in that culture has become psychiatrized to such an extent that conditions that were previously assimilated in communities are now diagnosed as psychotic conditions. In reverse, too, behaviors that were previously considered abnormal, such as deviant sexual practices, are now considered alternative life-styles. For example, a patient in one hospital discovered for himself that the thing that kept him in the hospital was his insistence that he regularly experienced mystical visions of the "light of God" guiding his actions. No adverse social effects were associated with these visions hindering the freedom of others. Yet, when asked, he obediently told his physician that he had these visions, until one day he discovered that this was his own private business. Then he ceased to tell the doctor. Much to his surprise he was dismissed within five days after he ceased to tell his physician about his visions of God. The problem of informing the physician is the obverse side of the physician informing the patient!

4. The Patient's Right to Privacy. The reference to the patient's discovery that his eccentric patterns of thinking were his own private business raises a basic ethical issue being debated among psychotherapists of the existential tradition as over against the behavioral therapists of the Skinnerian tradition: Does a human being have a private self, or is a human being the sum total of his "external" behaviors, to paraphrase Kant. Kant spoke often of the "privatus intellectus" which characterizes the human person. Skinner rejects this idea as he says: "It is tempting to attribute the visible behavior to another organism inside—to a little man or homunculus. The wishes of the little man become the acts of the man observed by his fellows. The inner idea is put into words." Concepts such as the "soul" and "the self" are ways of describing the "little man" or the "homunculus."[17]

When we view this debate between Skinner and Carl Rogers, we are likely to be drawn into the great battle as to whether man is a living soul. I believe that man is, not has, a soul. In the Hebrew tradition I believe that this involves mankind's total, unified being with integrity. That is not the issue, here, however. The issue in terms of a person's freedom is: Does a person have a right to his or her own private thoughts? The patient described above discovered that his own private relationship to God was his own private business! We cannot effectively discuss the ethics of the invasion of a person's privacy through behavioral control methods described in this paper until we come to the conclusion that the patient *has* privacy by the nature of his or her own thought process. I have not seen this issue discussed in the literature on the ethics of behavior control.

5. Minimal versus Maximum Goals for Human Behavior. Another critical issue in the ethics of behavior control concerns the quality or extent of goals for the human person. In treatment situations, the goals are minimal and have been stated as the survival of the person as one who is able to behave in such a way that he or she is able to survive at a minimum in terms of eating, sleeping, housing, clothing for himself, and working to such an extent that these needs are met without undue dependency on others. However, these are least-common-denominator goals for human existence, albeit they are prerequisite to any others. The Christian faith subordinates these minimal needs to a supreme, maximal goal. That goal is placing the survival of our neighbor above that of ourselves, that is loving one's neighbor as oneself (a Jewish ideal) and even more, loving one another as Christ loved us and gave himself for us.

The maximum goal of psychotherapy at its best is, as Harry Stack Sullivan put it, to enable a person to the kind of maturity in which he or she can love another person as much as, or almost as much as, oneself. When we read this, we think that this person is not far from the kingdom of God. As I have experienced psychiatrists, psychotherapists, and behavioral therapists in the setting in which I work, I find a quiet, nondenominational commitment to this higher goal for therapy. As a Christian, I would explicitly say that an even higher expectation of self-sacrificing love over and above simply providing freedom in coexistence, according to Kant, is the summum bonum of goal selection for behavior modification, even for churches themselves.

6. The Restoration of Creation. Some of the somatic therapies which have been described in this paper can specifically be seen as restoring the organism of a person to the original purpose of its creation. For example, the diabetic, with insulin supplementation wisely administered and conscientiously taken, can live a normal life. The question is being raised as to whether some of the symptoms of chronic depression and mania may not be in this same way treated. If a given psychotropic drug is a specific and demonstrable supplement to the body chemistry, then is this a restoration of the creation as it was originally intended to work?

When we ask such questions, the answer is yet a mystery. We have been formed in the secret wisdom of God whose eyes beheld our unformed substance when as yet there was none of them. Such knowledge is too wonderful for us. Yet, we have been given the technology to search after the knowledge of the true state of our own being.

As we see the mysteries of the human organism being revealed to us, we can say: "O God, these are your thoughts we are thinking after you!" Or, we have other more self-centered options. God grant that we will know that knowledge is surpassed by self-sacrificing therapeutic wisdom and our best humanity lies beyond our own survival.

Notes

[1] Immanuel Kant, *The Science of Right.* Great Books Series, vol. 49, p. 398.

[2] "Conditioning and Other Technologies Used to 'Treat?' 'Rehabilitate?' 'Demolish?' Prisoners and Mental Patients," *Southern California Law Review* (1972) 45:616–684.

[3] Frank Carrera, III, M.D., and Paul L. Adams, M.D., "An Ethical Perspective on Operant Conditioning," *Journal of American Academy of Child Psychiatry*, vol. 9 (October, 1970), no. 4, p. 609.

[4] William Glasser, *Reality Therapy* (New York: Harper & Row, 1965).

[5] Jerome K. Myers and Lee L. Bean, *A Decade Later: A Follow-Up of Social Class and Mental Illness* (New York: John Wiley, 1968), pp. 97–98.

[6] Freedman, Kaplan, and Sadock, *Comprehensive Psychiatry II. Second Edition* (Baltimore: William Wilkins), vol. 2, p. 1982.

[7] Eliot S. Valenstein, *Brain Control: A Critical Examination of Brain Stimulation*

and Psychosurgery (New York: John Wiley, 1973), pp. 210 ff..

[8] Ibid., p. 142.

[9] B. F. Skinner, *Science and Human Behavior* (New York: Free Press, 1953), p. 353.

[10] The American Psychiatric Association, *Task Force Report on Behavior Therapy in Psychiatry* (New York: Jason Aaronson, 1974), pp. 97–105.

[11] B. F. Skinner, *Beyond Freedom and Dignity* (New York: A. A. Knopf, 1971), p. 104.

[12] Philip Roos, "Human Rights and Behavior Modification," *Mental Retardation*, vol. 12, no. 3 (June 1974), pp. 3–6.

[13] Bruce J. Ennis, "Civil Liberties and Mental Illness," *Criminal Law Bulletin*, vol. 7, no. 2 (1971), pp. 101–127.

[14] Frank Carrera and Paul Adams, "An Ethical Perspective on Operant Conditioning," *Journal of the American Academy of Child Psychiatry*, vol. 9, no. 4 (October 1970), pp. 607–623. Buhler quoted here also.

[15] World Medical Association, 1964, *Declaration of Helsinki: Human Experimentation*.

[16] Seymour L. Halleck, "Legal and Ethical Aspects of Behavior Control," *The American Journal of Psychiatry*, 131:4 (April, 1974), pp. 381–385.

[17] T. W. Wann, ed., *Behaviorism and Phenomenology* (Chicago: University of Chicago Press, 1964), pp. 79–80.

4
Christian Ethics
And Biomedical Issues:
A Physician's Perspective
George E. Duncan

In this chapter Dr. George E. Duncan writes about several selected biomedical issues: (1) kidney transplants; (2) the use of the dialyzer; and, (3) heart transplants. In the process he also deals with a definition of death from a medical and legal point of view.

This chapter, along with the two chapters that follow, results from a panel discussion held at the Christian Life Commission conference on Biomedical Ethics. In this panel a physician, pastor, and hospital chaplain discussed biomedical issues.

The ideas that Dr. Duncan shares here grow out of his active involvement in both religion and medicine in his community. He has tirelessly encouraged and worked for dialogue between people in medicine and religion.

Dr. Duncan has been in the private practice of surgery in Nashville, Tennessee for more than a quarter of a century. Since 1951 he has also served as a clinical instructor in the Department of Surgery at Vanderbilt University Medical School. He is a deacon in the First Baptist Church of Nashville where he is actively involved in the life of that community of believers. He has given strong leadership in a variety of church, professional, and community activities.

Christian Ethics
And Biomedical Issues:
A Physician's Perspective

One of the dramatic achievements in the field of medicine in the past two decades is the development of the use of anatomical transplants for diseased organs. This development has led to the surmounting of many technical difficulties in medicine, surgery, immunology, and biomedical engineering. The difficult problems are not limited to these fields, however, for as the techniques have developed and the knowledge we have has been applied, grave and difficult issues of a moral and ethical nature have evolved. Many different organs have been transplanted with more or less success and a number of different organs have been replaced by artificial substitutes. For the purpose of simplification, I will focus on the transplantation of the kidney, the use of the dialyzer, and heart transplants.

These drastic procedures compel attention to what is right and wrong for the individuals involved. What is right or wrong for the patient who is going to receive the transplant? What is right or wrong for the organ donor, be he a living donor or one who is dying? What is right or wrong for the members of the family? What is right or wrong for the professional team? What is right or wrong for society at large?

A patient afflicted with impending death from organ failure has every right to seek and consent to any measure which will prolong his life and alleviate his suffering. In making the decision as to whether or not to receive a transplant, he must know what the chance of success for the transplant is, versus the financial difficulty he will have, and the physical and mental suffering he must undergo. In the past ten years the chance of success from a kidney transplant has risen from just 5 percent to 80 percent due to improvement in the understanding of the process of autoimmunization and the technique of the operation itself. A patient can be maintained on dialysis for an indefinite period of time. Yet, the quality of that life may leave something to be desired. The cost of the kidney transplant is in the neighborhood of $20,000. The cost of dialysis is about $150 each time the machine is used, which runs between $5,000 and $8,000 a year. At present all the individuals who receive transplants or who are accepted for dialysis are covered under Medicare.

What is right or wrong for the living donor? Persons who give one of their healthy kidneys to a dying patient perform an admirable, generous, and courageous act. But he must be under no unusual external pressure to donate his kidney. The surgical mortality for the donor is less than one-tenth of one percent. He does assume some additional risk because something might happen to his other kidney and he may need to be a transplant patient himself. This does not happen often.

The donor needs to avoid a feeling of guilt if the transplant does not work. If the patient dies, frequently the donor feels that something must have been wrong with him or it would have worked. Many experience these feelings if there is a close relationship between donor and recipient. These possible physiological and psychological hazards are not great but the physician and donor must know about them so they can be minimized.

What about the dying donor? The greatest hope in the future for securing enough kidneys for persons needing transplants lies in the use of the kidneys of dead people. Ethical issues mentioned above really do not apply here, but other issues arise. The dying potential donor must receive every care that is available to him as an individual. He needs to be under the care of a medical team that is independent of the medical team that is going to do the transplant itself.

For a kidney to be usable it must be obtained within an hour after death. Here the definition of death becomes crucial. In some states the patient has died when he has stopped breathing for ten minutes. In others death is present when the heart stops beating. In Tennessee, for example, you are dead when the doctor says you are dead. This is the law. Now, whether it is a respiratory death or whether it is death from cardiac failure, brain death is always involved. Increasingly there is the belief by many people that the patient is dead when his brain ceases to function. Great efforts are being made to establish reliable criteria for brain death. Legal rulings on this matter are slow in being made and the acceptance of brain death as final is by no means widely accepted.

What is brain death? Prominent among the criteria for brain death are these four things: First, when there is a deep, irreversible coma as in the Karen Quinlan case. Second, when there is a persistent flat electroencephalogram. Karen Quinlan did not have this at the time when her parents were first involved in legal proceedings related to their decision to remove her from the life support system. Third, when there is no sign of respiration after mechanical assistance is stopped. It was thought that after assistance was stopped, Karen would die. It was stopped and she did not die. Fourth, when there is the absence of the pupillary and tendon reflexes. Better methods of establishing brain death might be found as neurochemical analyses are developed. These analyses are not yet reliable.

What is right or wrong for the families of recipients and donors? Families of patients whose lives are prolonged by mechanical means undergo many stresses and tensions. They should not be given over-enthusiastic expectations of good results any more than the patient should be given high expectations for the results of the transplant. These operations offer hope for the patient but there are no guarantees. It is the doctor's responsibility to avoid excessive pressure on the family to give a kidney because fears and guilt feelings following the surgery for individuals who do not want to be donors must be prevented. The press and lay-science writers need to educate the public in a responsible manner about these things. The Uniform Anatomical Gift Act should be supported whereby a person who is still in good health can make organs available at the time of death.

What is right or wrong for the medical team? Dialyzers, available organs, and teams for doing transplants, have been in limited supply. The decision as to who gets the machine raises difficult ethical questions for the doctors to answer. In Seattle when this work was first started and uremic patients were being treated, the help of an anonymous committee was enlisted. The committee chose which patients' lives should be saved. This resulted in assigning certain worth to certain lives, a procedure ethically and religiously repugnant to many. Other teams avoid the problem by making kidneys available on a first-come-first-serve basis. It is hard for the team to avoid assigning certain values to certain lives—the young versus the old, the talented versus the untalented, the family breadwinner versus the bum on skidrow.

The solution perhaps is to make this treatment available to all who need it. When you consider the cost and time and the need for experimentation in other fields where more common diseases may be treated the expenses of kidney transplants is questioned. The number of teams is increasing. The number of dialyzers is increasing and the supply of kidneys is increasing. So perhaps this problem is already in the process of being solved.

The medical profession has gone to great lengths to try to establish guidelines that will cover transplant patients. Recently the Committee on Morals and Ethics of the Transplantation Society has made some pertinent statements regarding organ transplants. A summary of those statements are as follows: Renal transplants are a therapeutic procedure and are widely successful in the hands of trained teams. Transplantation of other organs is acceptable as an experimental procedure.[1]

The heart transplant requires continuing study. The risk to the recipient must be weighed against the benefits. The health of the living donor is paramount. Cadaveric sources of organs is desirable morally and otherwise. The death of the prospective cadaveric donor must be certified by two physicians who are not members of the transplant team. The transplant of organs of other mammals is an acceptable experimental procedure. The sale of human organs is indefensible according to these criteria. The privacy of the donor and of the recipient must be respected.

Finally, what is right or wrong for society? If society is going to support research in the field of transplants and the application of the knowledge that we have, they must be kept informed. We need cooperation between the medical community and the responsible press. The rights of patients to privacy versus the right of the public to know has been debated for centuries. And the debate has not been decided. Now, funds for health care must compete in the public arena with funds for education, housing, transportation, welfare, antipoverty programs, and national defense.

Choices, priorities, ethical and moral decisions will continue to be made on an individual basis. Improvements in technology and equipment, and knowledge of the rejection phenomena surely will take place. Continued progress in worthwhile achievement will certainly evolve when these emphases proceed.

Notes

[1] Merrill, J. P. 1971—Statement of the Committee on Moral and Ethics of the Transplantation Society. *Annual of Internal Medicine*, 75: 631–633.

5
Christian Ethics
And Biomedical Issues:
A Pastor's Perspective
David C. George

Dr. George explores here the exercise of responsibility which must accompany the progress that has been made in biomedical technology. He relates these matters to his experience as a pastor with preaching and counseling responsibilities.

There are helpful insights developed here about the role of the pastor in the decision-making process. Dr. George is a gifted pastor who calls for pastors to give abundant help to people who must make biomedical decisions. He calls for the pastor to be an enabler in the process so that people will have the ability to make these decisions themselves.

David C. George is pastor of the Immanuel Baptist Church in Nashville, Tennessee. He did his college work at Howard Payne College in Brownwood, Texas. His seminary work was done at Southwestern Baptist Theological Seminary where he received his Th.D. degree. Active in denominational life, Dr. George has also been deeply involved in community activities. This chapter comes from a pastor who is both a strong preacher and a sensitive, understanding counselor.

Christian Ethics
And Biomedical Issues:
A Pastor's Perspective

One of the greatest blessings of our time has been the progress of medical technology, but this very progress has placed on us the awesome burden of freedom and the responsibilities that go with such freedom. As a pastor, I have been called to help people find their freedom and fulfill their responsibilities in the light of God's purpose. If biomedical developments present new options for freedom and raise new questions about moral responsibility, then these are pastoral problems. The pastor must help individuals and institutions view these matters in the light of the will of God.

We seem to have been taken by surprise by many of these issues. They have developed so rapidly. Many of the problems seem exotic and far-removed from our experience, but I have already observed that today's exotic possibility may come walking in the pastor's door tomorrow or may be encountered in a hospital room within twenty-four hours. The world is moving fast, especially in the area of science. Anyone who deals with the total range of human life as the pastor does must be prepared.

There have been some problems in the Christian community which have led us to fail to develop a climate of informed concern about issues related to biomedical ethics. The Southern Baptist Christian Life Commission has done a fine job in helping remedy this through its conference on biomedical ethics. There has also been some failure in the medical and scientific community to see the patient as a whole person who is part of a community, a family, and a church. Sometimes the parishioner-pastor relationship has been ignored, and the pastor hears about these biomedical, ethical questions after the decision has been made. There are many reasons for this, but some of them are built into the system and they need to be changed.

One issue which every pastor must deal with, either directly or indirectly, is abortion. In my experience, women considering abortion usually do not consult the pastor. This may reflect a lack of openness on the part of many pastors and a corresponding lack of trust on the part of parishioners. But even in the best of pastoral relationships, abortion is, first of all, a woman's problem and a very private and sensitive problem.

Whether the issue arises in a direct counseling relationship, in dealing with other family members and physicians, or in the ministry of preaching and teaching, it is a matter that deserves much thought and prayer by the pastor. I think the pastor must resist the temptation to make people's decisions for them, but he needs to give his people a lot of help for making their decisions. This help should be given early. The time of crisis is usually too late to start forming attitudes for Christian decision making.

More frequent and more open opportunities come to the pastor as he ministers to people facing medical crises. One issue that has troubled me is the question of communication between medical professionals, patients, families, and ministers. I have been particularly frustrated in trying to minister to the dying. They suspect it, they fear it, they gradually begin to realize it; but by the time they could really understand that their life is about to end, they are sedated and encumbered with medical equipment. This means there is seldom any meaningful communication in the process. I have watched a number of people die without ever really meeting them on an honest, person-to-person level. I do not know how to solve this problem, but I think the issue of communication and truth-telling is a serious issue.

As a pastor, I am concerned about the larger question of the delivery of health care. I have seen individuals come back from distant medical centers and famous surgeons with bills for thousands of dollars which their insurance companies paid. And I have seen families who got very little medical care. I have seen a poor family lose an infant to a congenital heart defect without ever having the benefits of modern heart surgery. I have known a young widow who went deeply in debt during her husband's dying days in the hospital. Modern medicine has wonderful benefits, but they are not yet evenly distributed.

How does a pastor help people who are involved in the medical care process? I think education is the basic way. I have come more and more to feel that the time of crisis is too late to educate. I have tried to deal with the youth of my church to prepare them for marriage, for parenthood, for future suffering and illness, and for many of life's other situations.

We need to lead people to view all of life in a Christian perspective. One-to-one counseling is important, but equally important is the network of relationships we help to build around people. In our society many isolated families encounter these decisions without anyone to sit down and talk it over with them. There is a growing need for the church to be a supporting, informed, loving community that can help people make decisions about the issues of life, including biomedical issues.

There are certain principles we can follow. L. Harold DeWolfe, in the title of his book, *Responsible Freedom,* has indicated the basic one. I want my people to know that God has given us freedom, and he holds us responsible for the way we exercise it. This freedom means it is not wrong to do new things, even though they have never been done before, or to do things which are artificial—in the sense that they involve means not already present in the process of nature. God has given us knowledge, wisdom, and skill, and we are free to use them.

On the other hand, we must lead people to exercise their freedom with a sensitive conscience. Sensitizing the conscience may give a person more of a burden instead of less of a burden, but it is still necessary. It is alarming how many people are making the decision for abortion, for example, with apparent disregard for the seriousness of the moral decisions they are making.

Along with the sense of responsibility, we must also communicate a sense of grace and forgiveness. We must let people know that once they make a responsible decision, they can live boldly and with confidence. A well-made decision may not be a perfect decision, but the grace of God still operates in our lives.

Above all, I hope to lead my church to be a redemptive, supportive community for patients and also for medical professionals in the church. I have seen doctors who have become calloused and hardened by the weight of the matters they are handling. I hope the church can provide all who are involved in biomedical decision making with the information, inspiration, and encouragement they need to live before God in responsible freedom.

6
Christian Ethics and Biomedical Issues: A Chaplain's Perspective

William C. Mays

As a hospital chaplain William C. Mays writes about several issues that he deals with as a part of his professional responsibilities. First, he looks at the difficult matter of euthanasia. Second, he explores his views on death with dignity. He gives attention to the need for dialogue between people in medicine and religion. Finally, Dr. Mays discusses the problems related to conflicts of interest in the medical community.

This chapter reflects the views of one who is involved daily in matters of life and death. These words reflect the life and thought of one who combines gentleness of spirit with moral firmness—a happy combination.

Dr. Mays serves as chaplain and director of Pastoral Services and Education at the Baptist Hospital in Nashville, Tennessee. He has been in this position since 1965. He is also Base Chaplain for the Tennessee Air National Guard. And he is a visiting lecturer at Vanderbilt Divinity School. Dr. Mays is active in Immanuel Baptist Church, Nashville, where he serves as a Sunday School teacher. He has written articles for both religious and medical publications.

Christian Ethics and Biomedical Issues: A Chaplain's Perspective

The field of biomedical ethics is so broad and complex that it defies simple definition and resists comprehensive treatment. It is only possible then, due to the limitation of space, to treat one issue somewhat exhaustively or to hold up several issues in a brief and suggestive manner. Because of personal concerns and interests, I have chosen the latter course. As a hospital chaplain, my perspective is clinical rather than theoretical. I reflect the environment in which I work and minister daily.

Consider first the matter of euthanasia. A survey of the literature in the field reveals that euthanasia is often defined in both an active and passive sense. Active euthanasia is understood as a deliberate, willful act of ending the life of a suffering person. Passive euthanasia is an act of omission that results in the death of the patient. Both types of euthanasia are further subgrouped into voluntary and involuntary categories. An example of active voluntary euthanasia is suicide; active involuntary is the action of the physician or some other person to terminate the patient's life.

To pull the plug of the bird respirator, to administer a massive overdose of morphine, these are active procedures that I cannot support. But I do affirm euthanasia in the voluntary passive sense. I support the individual rights of a patient who signs the so-called "Living Will" or the person who says to his physician and others who care for him physically, "I don't want any heroics done on me. When my heart stops, let me go. Don't use emergency means to bring me back." I support involuntary passive euthanasia when understood as the physician's and/or family's decision that no heroics be implemented on a patient unable to make the decision himself.

This, from my perspective, is more of a gut reaction than a well-thought-out theoretical stance. But let me share with you two or three brief reasons why I stand where I do on this issue. First, I think it is *humane*. Most of us are for shooting a horse with a broken leg. We support taking Fido when he is fifteen years old, blind, and lame to the vet and allowing the appropriate shot to be given. I am not suggesting that we do this with human beings, but I am suggesting that it is humane to allow a terminally ill patient who has lost his ability to live meaningfully to die a natural death. I think it is humane.

Secondly, I believe it is *Christian*. To me, my understanding of Christian living is life with meaningful, interpersonal relationships with other people and a deep personal relationship with God. I would suggest to you that there are those times in a general hospital when you see terminally ill patients come to the place in life when they no longer have meaningful interpersonal relations and where, I think, only from God's side do they have a meaningful religious relationship. They cannot pray, they cannot read the Bible, they cannot think in terms of their relationship to God. They are past this. I would suggest to you that from a Christian standpoint meaningful life is over, is ended, and we can well let such a person die as he will.

In the third place, I support passive euthanasia for *financial* reasons. Are you aware of how much it costs to keep somebody alive for an extra day, an extra week, an extra month? It is my observation that many physicians wish to disclaim financial considerations as a part of their responsibility. This last year in a Clinical Pastoral Education program conducted in our hospital, one of our fine neurosurgeons was invited to speak to our training group. We raised the financial question with him and he responded, "That's not my responsibility. I order the best care and then the family and/or society must pay for that care. It is not my responsibility to consider the financial status of the family." I do not think it is only the physician's responsibility, but I do believe he shares this responsibility with many others. Let me illustrate with an experience a friend shared with me.

A man's wife was dying in the intensive care unit of a general hospital. The man and the primary physician agreed that no heroic measures would be used to extend her life. This was agreeable to both of them. The woman was in the final days of her life. The primary physician, however, left town for the weekend, leaving a resident doctor in charge. The resident came in, full of youthful enthusiasm, read the chart, turned to the head nurse, and began ordering a battery of procedures, medicines, and machines.

When the husband arrived for regular visiting hours, he found his wife surrounded by machinery and energetically working people. He said, "No, this is not what I want. The doctor and I had agreed that this would not happen." Whereupon he was royally dressed down by the resident physician. The man insisted, "I can't afford it. I can't pay for it. You are running up my bill, and I will not be able to take care of the expense." Again, the doctor turned on him with great anger, saying, "It is my duty to do everything I can to help this person, and you are selfish to think only of money." I would suggest to you that this conversation ought never to have taken place, that there *is* an implicit responsibility for financial consideration in such circumstances.

In the second place, and I want to look at this issue briefly, I am for *death with dignity*. As good as modern medical practice is in this country, I do not think what we experience is always dignified. I do not believe that some of the procedures and some of the equipment used are those which make the last few hours of life most meaningful. I am convinced also that some of our intensive care units are more for the convenience of our hospital personnel and our medical staff than they are either for the good of the patient or for his family.

Let me give you one illustration that happened recently. A young man in his early twenties was dying. The doctor knew he was dying and communicated this to the family. The patient, however, remained in a medical intensive care unit. His family was eating and sleeping in a family waiting room twenty-four hours a day and getting in to see him for only five minutes every three or four hours.

My question is, why could he not have died just as well in a private room where his family might have been around him? I think this would have brought dignity to his dying.

The third biomedical issue I want to focus on can be illustrated by a couple of personal experiences. Some months ago I was sitting in the doctor's lounge in our hospital and I overheard a very interesting discussion. Some of our physicians were talking about a particular law they were involved in writing for consideration by the state legislature. It was a law dealing with certain moral and ethical issues in medical practice in this state. I guess rather naively I asked, "Who else is on your committee besides doctors?" And I got an incredulous look and the physician said, "Nobody." So I asked, "Well, have you thought of some outstanding clergyman in this community who has the training in the field of morality and ethics that you might pull in for your committee?" And he replied, "It's nobody's business but ours until it becomes law."

You will recall that when the Supreme Court made their so-called liberal decision regarding the abortion issue that this forced many of us to take a new look at the question. The hospital where I worked was no exception. We needed to come up with some statement regarding our policy on abortion to give to the news media and also to satisfy patients and staff. It was very interesting to me that when the statement was being written I was asked for what information I had in my library, but I was not asked for an opinion or any input in the matter.

Now, what I am saying in these two examples is exactly what I think Dr. Daniel McGee has said elsewhere in this book. I was not more able to write the abortion statement than the administrator chosen. But I think moral and ethical laws and statements of policy require more than one perspective. They need perspectives from many different professions and vocations. And so far, at least in many communities, this is not being done.

In the last place, I want to focus on something that may be both unpopular and highly controversial. I am getting more and more concerned about a *conflict of interests* that I see going on in the medical communities all across our nation. Investor-type hospital corporations are springing up in many cities. They are building new hospitals and buying others. I think there is some very positive good that has come out of this movement. This is an American free enterprise undertaking in the best sense of the term. And because these people want to turn a profit for their stockholders, they are going to learn the very best methods for delivering health care. From that standpoint, I think it is positive.

I must raise one bothersome, questionable issue, however, and that is the fact that in many communities physicians have become major stockholders in some of these corporations. I suggest to you that it becomes a conflict of interests when a doctor must decide whether he should admit a patient to a hospital which he partially owns or to one in which he owns no stock. I suggest the temptation exists as to whether you send the patient where he gets the best care, where the best equipment is available, where the best kind of treatment is given, or whether you send him where ultimately you help yourself.

These comments are no more than suggestive. Like the tip of the proverbial iceberg, they give little evidence of the depths beneath. It is my hope that they will be prods to your further reflection and study.

7
Biomedical Issues And Reproduction
Kenneth L. Vaux

Decisions that will be made about technology and reproduction are going to have a profound impact on the human race. The writer of this chapter speaks to the issues from his experience as a pastor and an ethicist.

Dr. Vaux warns us of some of the dangers we face in this field. He calls for the development of an ethic broad enough to speak to the issues that the future will hurl at us. He believes that biomedical ethics must be dealt with by the church with an emphasis on the preciousness and inviolability of each human individual.

Dr. Vaux serves as professor of ethics and theology at the Institute of Religion, Texas Medical Center, Houston, Texas. He is an ordained minister, having served churches as pastor and as minister of education. Dr. Vaux is adjunct associate professor of law at the University of Houston and also teaches ethics at Baylor College of Medicine's Department of Psychiatry and Department of Community Medicine. Dr. Vaux has published widely and his book *Biomedical Ethics: The Morality of Medicine* is a basic work in this field. He speaks frequently at national forums, conferences, and workshops on biomedical issues.

Biomedical Issues
And Reproduction

At this point in American history a special destiny awaits the noble tradition of the Southern Baptist Convention because we need to blend so uniquely the puritan and enthusiast strains in our religious culture. America yearns for an evangelical revival. No moral regeneration can come except from a spiritual awakening. The symbolic meaning of the political trauma and restoration we have moved through in recent months may bear this meaning. But the Southern Baptist Convention, indeed evangelical Christendom in general, is in grave danger of missing its opportunity because of its apathy towards the biomedical issues. That is why something very important is signified by the conference of the Christian Life Commission on biomedical ethics.

Senator Kennedy is absolutely correct when he says that the most important political issues for the remaining years of this century will be bioethical issues. Certainly they are the most important moral issues that we will face. The Roman Catholics have given intensive attention to the issues of sexuality, reproduction, family planning, and family life. But where among Protestants is the concern for a vision of human life, of human generativity, of life together? Where are those moral impulses that are built upon a biblical sense of the preciousness of bodily life, of life together, and death of the body? Helmut Thielicke has felt for many years that the great abdication of evangelical Christendom has been its retreat from the issues of bios and eros—of man's biological life in birth and in procreation and in dying.

In the ten years I have been working with these issues, the

Christian Life Commission conference on biomedical ethics marks the first time I have ever been asked to address these issues from a specifically Christian commitment. I have been in the political forums, all of the national institutes and agencies, and I have never had this opportunity, nor have I ever really sensed the freedom to say it like I want to say it.

Our starting point is religious ethics, specifically Christian ethics. I quite disagree with those who say that we must filter out that common denominator that could be called a natural rationalistic ethic and make that normative in our country. It seems to me to render absurd the Christian claims for truth. If something is true for a Roman Catholic, it must be true. If something is true for a Southern Baptist, it must be true for all.

A Christian view implies a peculiar vision of life, a radically unique sense of meaning and valuation. But what do we do with this in the midst of a secularized, pluralistic world? One option is a retreat ethic. It is stated sometimes in very shallow terms, sometimes very profoundly. William Stringfellow calls it "an alien ethic in a strange land." Perhaps this is our task. Perhaps the world has gone so far that this is the only posture to take—"an alien retreat, ghetto, Dead Sea cave-type ethic." Perhaps we need radically different senses of the meaning of life in these small cells in the midst of a dying culture. Perhaps the thing for the Christian community to do today is to abandon the fallen world to its own folly.

This probably would be the preferred option were it not for one fact—that Christ died in the world, for the world, at the hands of the world. He illustrated God's love for the world. He came not to condemn the world but to heal the world, to save the world. Our ethic is rooted in the enduring meaning he brings to the world. He is the ongoing signal to us of the will of God in our crises of decisions. He is normative man. He is making a new person, a new community, a new humanity, and a new creation. To me that's the only normative structure upon which a Christian can think about biomedical ethics.

Some say that there are no norms, that one value is as good as another since all are relative. Some absolutize penultimate judgments, codes, social mores, and moralistic hang-ups: and in making these absolute we ridicule Christian ethics in the eyes of the world. Some transmute our basic psychic, emotive, and ideological hang-ups into moralisms and cause the world to say, "If that's Christian, count me out!"

I want to consider the responsibility we have in the light of this theological context of bringing children into the world, of reproduction. The essence of the Christian ethic in this field, I would say, is the preciousness and inviolability of each person. That would mean each person yet to be born, each person newly born, each living and breathing person, and each infirm and dying person. The radical ethic of Christianity goes beyond this. Even John Rawls notes in his book, *A Theory of Justice,* that there is a particular and intense obligation we have to those who are most vulnerable—the least of these—"those in original position." In Rawls' language, there are those who we are so tempted to consider as burdensome and expendable. This single value demands of us that we initiate measures to insure growth and opportunity for each life, and, negatively, it prompts prescriptions limiting violations and harmful manipulation of persons. I want to look at the problems of generativity and reproductive biology.

First, I want to refer to a case which has been in the news. It is paradigmatic. It speaks to the situation that we are all in. In the little northern Alpine town of Stevezo, Italy, a moral anguish now grips the hearts of many young families. Recently, a dangerous cloud of poisonous gas was released over a chemical company just north of Milan. People knew something was wrong when the mice, then the cats, and then the dogs started dying. (We always send in the animals before us. We allow a bird to fly down into a mine. If the bird comes flying out, you know it's safe for men to go in. As in Genesis, animals are the sentinels of man. They live and die for his good. He names them in dominion.) In Stevezo, very soon, many of the young mothers, including those who were pregnant, became exposed to this gas. For the most part they were devout, rural Roman Catholics. But they faced the possibility that the life they carried in their bodies might be adversely affected—slightly or greatly.

In this instance there is something that is representative of the dilemmas we face—incomplete knowledge. Several mothers have already gone to Milan for abortions. Others are torn in their consciences over the moral choice they face. The Church says that it is wrong to have an abortion, even in this case, but it ministers to those who feel they must do it. It is a profoundly ambivalent and torn situation.

It points to several things we face now as individuals, as churches, as nations. One is the new burden of knowledge and technology. I would like to outline that first. Second is the correlative fall from innocence which is also an ascent into power and responsibility that is terrifying. And then there remains an enduring ambiguity about the choices we face and what is genuinely moral to do. And finally, we have to decide fast—before five o'clock this afternoon—that's what real moral choices are like.

Consider that outline in the light of these reproductive developments: First, the knowledge and technology. It has been outlined very lucidly by Dr. Stumpf (see Chapter 10). In addition, the technology I sketch is just around the corner. It is partially in use right now. It is partially on the drawing board, but in five years it will be routine. Amniocentesis is no longer experimental. It was removed from the experimental treatments last spring by the National Institutes of Child Health Development when, after a study of three thousand women with an equal size control group, it was seen that there was less morbidity in those who had amniocentesis. There were less spontaneous abortions, less injuries to the fetus.

Amniocentesis is now rapidly becoming routine, especially for women who are older or where there is suspected genetically transmitted disease. In five years amniocentesis will be a regular part of maternal examinations for all pregnant women. This technique, along with the endocervical smear, is already being used for sexing—choosing the sex of your children. It is a very simple procedure. One just takes an endocervical smear from a woman who is suspected to be pregnant and illumines the "Y" chromosome. It is possible to tell whether she is pregnant with a boy or a girl. Given the *Roe* v. *Wade* abortion decision, some people will choose to have an abortion if they discover the fetus is the wrong sex. Persons can have abortions for any reason they choose now that this ruling is in effect.

The genetic tree can be drawn which will convey certain predictabilities to parents regarding the inheritance of their offspring. Fetoscopy and ultrasound will detect a wide range of gross disorders. Amniocentesis is now being augmented by a procedure called endoamnioscopy. An instrument which is inserted transvaginally takes not only cells which are sloughed off the fetus into the amniotic fluid but gets a blood sample from the little shoulder of the fetus and enables a wide range of chromosome and cell studies.

That's the technique and the technology, genetic knowledge combined with the antenatal diagnostic technology. What will they yield? Eventually multifaceted tests and lab work will make possible diagnosis on a wide scale for Downs Syndrome, the extra chromosome, mild or profound types of mental retardation and multibirth abnormalities that fill 50 to 70 percent of all our institutions for mental retardation in this country.

The Richmond School in Houston has fifteen hundred residents of which nine hundred are Mongoloid children. And, remember, all you can find is the chromosome abnormality. You cannot say where this is a profoundly diseased child or one who will be able to go through the university and become a professional. The same is true with sex discernment or a sex-linked disease. There is a growing list of inborn errors of metabolism, single gene disorders. Then there are the neural tube defects. When there is any little hole, a little aberration in that neural thread as it is developing, it throws off proteins, called Alpha fetal proteins, and when you find that you can suspect anencephaly, myelomelingocele, spina bifida. Sometimes you are right. Sometimes you are wrong. Sometimes it is a wee, little hole low in the spine. Sometimes it is a big hole high in the spine. But all you see are proteins. That's just the beginning.

The polygenetic disorders are beginning to be studied and show markers that can be diagnosed while in the fetal stage. Polygenetic disorders are just about everything that we have that will bring about death. These disorders have variable penetrance. Sometimes they go through and are devastating, sometimes they are not. Sometimes they yield only a predisposition to disease. Sometimes the disease presents itself.

Carcinoma of the breast, a major disease which affects women, is partly genetic in origin. It has genetic factors as do diabetes, arthritis, many forms of cancer, and heart disease. Certain studies are now homing in on the hyperlipoprotein diseases where something in your genes hampers the way that you process blood fats so that they build up and clog vessels. One day soon we will have readings of whether this fetus is likely to have a heart attack in his thirtieth or fortieth year, or develop childhood cancer or diabetes. Now these are very subtle markers and scientists will remind us that these are more evasive than I have suggested. But I am very impressed by how quickly the most conservative estimates are wiped out. Even Gordon Rattray Taylor in his book, *The Biological Time Bomb,* said, "By 1975, we will be able to choose the sex of our offspring." He was several years off, too conservative. And it's generally the case in science, particularly biomedical science.

Each of these problems present a question along with the general issue of elective abortion. And you know the questions! Is it worth spending $15,000 to discover one fetus with Downs Syndrome? Should we screen for carrier status in Tay-Sachs disease? Massive programs were started in every central city against sickle cell disease and then they were dropped because they were absurd. We've started screening programs in every city with massive Jewish populations and now we are dropping them. When you see dozens of twelve- and thirteen-year-old Jewish boys and girls already plagued with the thought of whether that girl or boy they just met in the hall at school is a carrier of Tay-Sachs disease, you get the tremendous emotional weight of this new knowledge. And we're up against the biblical sense of the burden of this knowledge—this exhilarating, liberating force—at once terrifying! It lifts you to heaven; it draws you down into hell.

One of my friends, named David, is five years old and he's in a bubble in Houston. He has one of those sex-linked problems, combined with a immuno-deficiency disease. His brother, born a year before him, had it and, like others all down through the ages, at about six months of age, started to develop massive infections after the maternal residue of immunity wore off. He didn't have any defenses and by the time he was rushed to the hospital, he was too far gone. So when David was born, they were ready with the bubble. David has been in that bubble ever since. He may come out. NASA is building him a portable bubble, space suit.

But his parents, and almost all other parents in this situation, are now deciding not to experiment. They do not want to know if a child will be born with this disease. More and more children with defects are being allowed to die. We are now coming around full circle tempered by realistic acceptance of boundaries.

You see the point. We are going to be presented with a partially colored portrait of the child and we must then decide whether to bring him into the world or not. Like those parents in Italy, it's only a very fuzzy picture with very little accuracy. All kinds of relativity regarding time and space and penetrance are present. We are all going to come to know what it means to be truly moral. It leaves us completely bewildered.

The policy questions are also profound. Does our ability to reproduce belong to us or to future generations? The "wrongful life" suits that Samuel Stumpf discusses (see Chapter 10) are a striking illustration of the moral ambivalence of our controls over future generations. Do we have an unlimited right to populate this planet? Do we have any right to exert birth control? That is a question with a greater depth than we generally realize.

Here is another big question. Should we begin to see genetic disease as communicable disease? The Communicable Disease Center has declared that genetic disease is communicable disease. It is transmitted even more predictably vertically rather than horizontally, like syphilis and measles. And, therefore, it should be quarantined.

I remember when my brother and I were sick as young boys, the health officials came and put a yellow sign up in our window: THIS HOUSE IS QUARANTINED. We don't do that too much anymore.

Some are saying that any measures necessary should be taken to insure that genetic diseases are not transmitted. Now, think back about the range, the spectrum of things that are genetic diseases. What does that mean?

Now, I would like to move to the emotional weight of this new knowledge and the moral ambivalence it creates. How are we going to use these new powers? We are learning very rapidly today how to keep a creative tension in our lives between resistance and acceptance and conquering those forces that hurt us and destroy us. Medicine at its root forces us to do theology again.

Dietrich Bonhoeffer once said, "We must learn to resist fate as resolutely as we learn to accept it at the right time." Teilhard, in a different way, says, "We must struggle against death with all our force for it is our fundamental duty as living creatures. But when, by virtue of a state of affairs unclear death takes us we must experience that strange paroxysm of faith in life whereby abandoning ourselves to death we fall into a greater life." Learning to live with that tension and paradox is the ethical challenge we face today.

A woman came into my office some time ago. Her husband was a medical doctor and, for some reason, their marriage wasn't going too well. After exploring whether this was just a routine occupational hazard, the woman poured out that she was not ready to commit herself, she was not ready to invest in and buy a home, she was not ready to have children, she had trouble generating any self-esteem or sense of purpose. I tried to get at what she was really saying. She skirted and rationalized until she finally blurted out in tears how her father had committed suicide in a state institution after many years of residing there as a paranoid schizophrenic. She assumed that the same fate awaited her. She was not willing to address herself to any risky thing—even life—because of what she suspected about herself. She had genetic hypochondria. It's a major disease in our world where a little knowledge is proving to be a dangerous thing.

We have all known Jewish and black friends who, during those unfortunate days of mass-required screening, were so scrupulous about their genetic attributes that they were hesitant to enter into any human interactions. A very wise man, named Kaspar Naegel, once said, "Health flourishes best when watched least." And a much wiser man said it differently with a much richer meaning, of course, when he said that he who saves his life will lose it (Matt. 16:35).

The second point in this emotional burden of ambiguity is the incapacity we have to accept pain and abnormality. The desire for perfection is very human, very much rooted in our thinking of who we are as biological creatures. Bentley Glass touches a deep feeling in us when he says that children have the right to be born normal. Just what does that mean? To wait outside the delivery room and to share the sigh of relief and joy when the nurse says, "Your baby is okay, and so is Mom," is to know this deep emotion. This natural and wholesome yearning for health and well-being is pushed to the absurd when we yearn for perfection. In fact, we know enough about disease, in particular mental disease, to know that if there's anything like perfection or if there's anything like intensely superb human nature, it is very close to what we have defined as illness. So what are we going to do when we identify an in-utero human being who will develop diabetes, cancer, heart disease, schizophrenia? I am afraid that our initial response may be a wholesale slaughter of unborn innocents. As long as we are obsessed, as we strangely are in this nation, with utopia, we run the grave danger of running roughshod over imperfection and, in the process, destroying that which is good in the human genius. Look how radically we have had to change our ideas of what it means to have a child with Downs Syndrome. In primitive German language a child with this disorder was called *Geschenk Gottep*—a gift of God. Likewise in Ireland, he was called *dinne L'dia*—God's gift. Now the child is seen as a tragic mistake. We didn't have the test in time. As the woman at Hopkins said, "You frittered around and you didn't give me the amniocentesis. The kid is yours. We're going home." And for fifteen days the doctors and nurses were forced to watch that child with Downs Syndrome starve to death because of duodenal atresia, an obstruction in the gut preventing processing of food.

Here we see a loss of innocence, a fall from innocence. We are again thrown back to our theology of health and disease, our theology of suffering. Will our passions for convenience and comfort and our shallow definitions of what is subnormal continue to prevail or will we recapture some sense of the infinite preciousness of each person, relatively deformed and diseased as we all are, and learn to watch with care over one another? This is the issue!

The theological issue is one of the most problematic—whether we can come up with some reinterpretation of all theology until the nineteenth century which said that pain and disease were visitations of God: "God whispers to us in joys, calls to us in our conscience, shouts to us in our pain." Helmut Thielicke says that the best way to conceive this theological question is to affirm that God does not cause disease, but nothing happens to you that has not passed before his eyes.

The first studies are coming in now on the use of these technologies. *The Journal of Chinese Medicine* this spring reports a study of one hundred amniocentesis in which fifty-three women were pregnant with boys and forty-seven with girls. One boy was aborted, twenty-nine girls were aborted. Do not think that male chauvinism is peculiarly a male syndrome.

The neonatal questions are always more difficult. Once a child sees the light of this world, once parents and nurses have touched the baby, have held the baby, you have a very different story. We must be able to accept the birth-defective child and find some other way to nurture and parent this child. More importantly, we have to find some way to energize the strength of our families to be caring and to be supportive. So when all is said and done, biomedical ethics falls right in the lap of the churches.

Ponder again the famous prayer of Reinhold Niebuhr. It seems to me to capture this blessed sense of being at once inquisitive, conquering, trying to overcome those forces detrimental to our well-being and at the same time accept the blessedness of the given: "Lord, give me the courage to change the things that can be changed, the patience to accept the things which cannot be changed, and wisdom to know the difference."

8
Christian Ethics
And Human Experimentation
Robert D. Reece

This chapter describes two well-known cases of medical experimentation and then discusses the light that Christianity sheds on the ethical issues involved in these cases. As a part of this discussion Dr. Reece explores the fundamental methodological question of how to derive principles of social ethics from the Bible and from Christian theology.

In his development of a Christian perspective on human experimentation, the author gives a succinct statement about the nature of Christian ethics. He explores several themes that are relevant to the two cases previously described. The chapter concludes with a look at Christian ethics and public policy, a matter of deep concern to all interested in biomedical issues.

Robert D. Reece is associate professor of Medical Ethics, Wright State University School of Medicine in Dayton, Ohio. He serves as chairman of the Department of Medicine in Society for the same institution. Dr. Reece was educated at Baylor University, Southern Baptist Theological Seminary, and Yale University where he received the Ph.D. in 1969. Dr. Reece is a brilliant teacher and he has taught in the fields of religion, law, and medicine. He is actively involved in the life of his church. In his writing and action he combines academic excellence with compassion for people who are in need.

Christian Ethics
And Human Experimentation

Nowhere is the dilemma of modern medicine more clearly apparent than in the area of experimentation involving human subjects. Scientific medicine has made great strides in recent decades in promoting health and relieving human suffering. The enormous progress in medicine in the last fifty years has been materially enhanced because of careful and extensive human experimentation. Because the results of an experiment can never be anticipated with certainty, the researcher is never certain that his experiment will not endanger the health and well-being of the subjects. This implies that the advance of medical knowledge, with all the potential benefits that new knowledge may provide for society at large, may sometimes be purchased at the expense of some individuals who suffer harm as a result of being experimental subjects. This contingency points to the basic dilemma inherent in medical research, since it can contradict medicine's intention to treat disease, relieve suffering, and promote health.

The area of human experimentation raises in a clear way the perennial question of the appropriate balance between the rights and welfare of the individual and the common good of society at large. I shall contend that the twin concepts of respect for the welfare and dignity of the individual and a dedication to the general welfare are at the heart of Christian social ethics. Although these principles are often complementary, they are also frequently in conflict. In cases of conflict, for example when a great social benefit may be gained by a research project involving high risk to the human subjects, an ethic rooted in the Christian tradition resists the easy sacrifice of the individual for the benefit of society at large. I shall further argue that the determination of whether a particular experiment is ethically defensible must not be left entirely to the discretion of the individual researcher, since experimentation on human beings is too important to be left solely to the experimenter. Instead it must be guided by principles and procedures that are established as public policy.

This chapter, which will be concerned with medical experimentation as opposed to behavioral or environmental research, will begin with an analysis of the ethical problems encountered in medical experimentation by describing two well-known and dramatic cases. These recent cases will highlight several of the ethical issues confronting both the researcher and those responsible for public policy. After I delineate the issues suggested by these two cases, I will consider what light the Christian tradition can shed upon our understanding of the ethics involved in these cases. In this chapter we will confront a fundamental methodological question; namely, how does one derive principles of social ethics from the biblical tradition and Christian theology. Proceeding in this way will lead to an understanding of the cases and will point the direction for appropriate public policy.

Two Representative Cases of Experimentation

The first case is the Public Health Service's Study of Untreated Syphilis in the Male Negro in Macon County, Alabama, more commonly known as the Tuskegee Syphilis Study.[1] The study began in 1932 when approximately four hundred black men in rural Alabama became part of a study of the long-term medical and psychological effects of untreated syphilis. They were subjects in this experiment without their knowledge and without their consent. The men were told that they had "bad blood" for which they were given injections for twenty-five years. The injections were placebos.

Even in the very early years of the study, the health of the group in virtually every medical category proved significantly poorer than the health of the group to which it was being compared. Even when the earlier drugs used in treating syphilis were superseded by the advent of a superior drug, penicillin, in the 1940s, no effort was made until 1966 to stop the experiment and provide available therapy to the survivors. It was not until public attention was focused on the study by a series of Associated Press articles in 1972 that a Department of Health, Education, and Welfare investigation effected the termination of the experiment.

The second example is of a very different sort. I refer not to a single study but to the general area of heart transplant surgery.[2] On December 3, 1967, the world was astonished by the announcement that Dr. Christian Barnard had performed the first transplant of a human heart into the body of another human being. Those familiar with the world of medicine, however, were neither surprised nor amazed. Prior animal work and successive stages of preliminary clinical investigation presaged this first transplant. The question was not whether such experimental surgery would be accomplished, but how soon and by whom. The first patient died eighteen days later, but long-term survival was achieved with Dr. Barnard's second transplant on Philip Blaiberg a month later.

The year of 1968 was heralded by the media as the year of the heart transplant, a daring adventure marking a symbolic victory involving the most culturally significant of the organs. But by the year's end, the evidence was already contradicting the early expressions of enthusiasm; it was becoming obvious that the technical success of the surgery itself was not matched by equal success in understanding and controlling the mechanism of tissue rejection. Regrettably the old quip was all too accurate: "the surgery was a success; unfortunately, the patient died."

November 1968 was the peak month for transplants; ironically, it was in that same month that a decision was reached which first signaled the rapid and radical decline of cardiac transplants. On November 30, the Montreal Heart Institute decided upon a moratorium on heart transplants to await further investigation into the failure of so many transplant procedures. By the time the moratorium was publicly announced two months later, only thirty-nine of the one-hundred eight recipients were still alive. Although many of the world's transplant surgeons objected to the Montreal moratorium, in fact, a dramatic slowdown of transplants occurred that amounted to a partial undeclared moratorium.

Autopsies indicated that patients died because of rejection episodes or through the efflorescence of infection brought about by large doses of immunosuppressive drugs prescribed to prevent rejection. The postmortem analysis of Dr. Blaiberg's death in August 1969 pointed to yet another problem in transplant surgery—the development of coronary artery disease in the recipient's new heart. Heart transplants and supporting research did continue, but a chastened, less ebullient group of transplanters proceeded more cautiously with less confidence of immediate victory. In 1969, the cardiac transplant experiment had reached a temporary dead end.

There are several features about these two cases which raise ethical questions. To say that a course of action is an ethical issue is not, of course, to make a prior moral judgment that it is ethically illegitimate, but simply that it is open to ethical investigation. This means that there are features about it and its relationship to particular values, rights, or obligations that warrant ethical analysis. The presumption that these two cases merit ethical examination presupposes that we bring to our first reading of them previous moral experience and some relevant system of moral principles.

In our society, for example, most of us would agree that generally one ought to attempt to relieve pain and suffering rather than inflict it, and that the arena for self-determination ought to be as extensive as possible. One ought to have a major voice in determining what is done to his person. We initially raise ethical questions about human experimentation because experimentation intersects so dramatically with these two general concepts.

Now, returning to larger issues emanating from the cases. Both cases arouse our moral sensitivity precisely because they are experiments rather than instances of standard medical practice. We tend to be conservative in our attitudes about medical practice; any significant departure from current practice must justify itself. This belief is so basic that even if current practice is discovered to be clearly harmful, we expect some evidence that a proposed new way of dealing with the issue will produce more good, or at least cause no more harm, than the old way, if it is to be adopted.

Both the syphilis study and the whole area of transplant surgery were undertaken presumably to develop new understanding and new therapies. Since they were experimental ventures into the as yet unknown, we intuitively want to ask whether life will be better or worse because of them. In both, while the questions reside within the public or collective consciousness, the burden of proof rests with the investigator.

In order to pose the ethical questions clearly, some comment on the nature and meaning of experimentation is necessary. To begin, the distinguishing characteristics of an experiment are its *intention* and its *methodology*. Interestingly, every office visit by a patient could be considered experimental, since the physician cannot know with absolute certainty how the standard therapy will affect this particular patient. It is therefore necessary to maintain a stricter definition which contrasts experimental medicine with accepted medical practice. Experiments are primarily for the purpose of gaining new knowledge; they typically require a research design that involves some degree of control to assure the validity and reliability of the data.

In light of this understanding, let us return to the cases. The Tuskegee case is clearly an example of experimentation. The intention and design of the study was research-oriented rather than therapeutic. Many are outraged that those four hundred people did not receive any medical treatment for their disease. Several mitigating factors should be noted in defense of the early investigations. The therapies available for syphilis in the 1930s were not exceptionally effective and were not without risks themselves. The experimental intent and design continued, however, even after a more effective treatment became available.

While experimental surgery does not lend itself to the same kind of experimental design, it remains clear that the physicians were engaged in a venture which would hopefully contribute new knowledge, new techniques, and new skills to the future of medical practice. Although there was not a strictly designated control group, the physicians' understanding of the experience of other patients suffering from similar diseases provided the basis for comparison with the subjects of their experiments.

The employment of a procedure or use of a medication which is experimental rather than established raises ethical questions for us. Moreover, our concern is greater because these cases represent instances of *experimentation* rather than *observational* research. An experimenter directly intervenes in the course of events, he introduces some control over a situation which changes its course in some way; in observational research the investigator is primarily a passive spectator. To cause something to happen renders the agent more responsible for its happening than if he merely observed it happening.

Clearly a heart transplant involves such direct and deliberate intervention; the surgeons can be either praised or blamed for their action. While it might be argued that the Tuskegee researchers were merely observing the blacks who already had the disease that was being studied, I would argue that by refraining from providing a therapy that was available, giving a placebo instead, the researchers were experimenting. Refraining from following a generally accepted procedure alters the course of events as significantly as initiating a new procedure. Any group which becomes part of an experiment, even if only as a control group, may have a moral claim upon the investigator; he should be concerned for their welfare and should prevent avoidable harm.

The common-sense principle that we ought to minimize pain suggests another important point about the two cases, which can be elucidated as the distinction between therapeutic and nontherapeutic experimentation. It would seem that it would be easier to justify an experiment that offers some prospect of therapeutic benefit for the subject of the experiment than one that does not. The more serious the risks to the subject and the less he has to gain from it personally, the more convincingly it must be defended ethically.

In the two cases under consideration, it would at the outset appear that the ultimate risks to the subjects were no greater than the risks of remaining untreated. The heart transplant recipients had serious coronary disease; they did not risk transplant surgery for relief of only mild heart disease. The patients in the Tuskegee study already had syphilis; the researchers did not give them syphilis in order to study them. However, there is a significant difference in the two cases in that the recipients of transplanted hearts could hope to be benefited by the "therapy"; there was no expectation that the group of four hundred black men in Tuskegee would benefit at all.

In retrospect, of course, it may well be that the cardiac patients suffered more because of the numerous reverses and crises in their medical condition than they would have had they simply died of their original disease—and they might have lived just as long without surgery, perhaps even more pleasantly. Likewise, although the experimenters did not give the men of Macon County syphilis, the fact that they were part of the study meant that they did not get treatment which they might have otherwise, and hence may have suffered more because of the experiment than they would have without it. The extent to which such results are foreseeable weigh heavily in ethical deliberations concerning such cases.

The final general comment about the nature of the ethical issues relevant for these cases derives from the principle of self-determination. Generally speaking, most of us feel that a man should have control over what is done to his body; he ought to be able to decide what treatment he receives, what experiments he accepts. It is noteworthy that the two cases contrast dramatically on this point. The patients in the transplant surgery cases consented to the transplants. They were physically free to consent; psychologically, they were as free as any man under a death sentence can be. The men in the Tuskegee study, by contrast, were not even told that they were part of an experiment. They thought they were receiving something to help their "bad blood." On the practical level, these concerns resolve themselves into the issue of informed consent, to which we shall return.

A Christian Perspective on Human Experimentation

Because these cases impinge upon some of our basic shared values they merit careful examination. The major focus of this essay, however, is what a specifically Christian ethic might say about such cases. The fundamental question is how a Christian ethic would even begin to address the issues. Some would even question whether there can be a Christian social ethic at all that could cope with problems of this sort. They argue that Jesus was only concerned with the relationships between individuals, and not at all with issues that involve the larger social institutions. Human experimentation is so far removed from anything that was considered by the biblical writers that the Bible cannot be expected to speak directly to this issue. Even the broad admonition to "Love your neighbor as yourself" provides no more than the beginning of a social ethic, since these words of Jesus give us little if any guidance in determining which neighbor we are to serve when there are limited benefits to be distributed among too many neighbors. The problem with experimentation is precisely that: many people may be benefited by knowledge gained in an experiment which may have harmed a few. Jesus' parable of the good Samaritan expands the range of who can be considered to be a neighbor, but it does not answer automatically for each specific case the question, Who is my neighbor?

The wellspring of Christian ethics is not exclusively the biblical tradition, since there is a long history of ethical reflection in the Christian tradition, which is part of the equipment of the contemporary Christian ethicist. The message of the Bible never comes to us bare, but is inevitably filtered through the lens of some particular theological perspective. There is no such thing as *the* Christian ethic. There are numerous ethics that claim the Christian banner, and though I find some more illuminating and more in accord with my understanding of the Christian faith than others, I would not be so presumptuous as to excommunicate any one of them. None can be dismissed, because each becomes a source of data to be used in the continuing task of Christian ethical reflection.

Christian ethics is the theological enterprise that draws from the wealth of biblical and Christian traditions in attempting to understand and interpret the contemporary world while seeking direction within the ever changing conditions of life.

As we look at that tradition, we can discern several themes which can help us formulate our thinking about human experimentation. My first observation has to do with the relational nature of Christian thought. Christian ethics is not in the first instance, a set of rules or laws or even a calculus for the impersonal calculation of competing values. Rather, Christian ethics is initially concerned with the right ordering of human relationships. Many of the key words of Christianity speak to relationships, relationships between man and God, and man and man—love, reconciliation, forgiveness, faith, and community.

From its biblical phase onward, much of the focus of Christian ethics has been on the life in community. H. Richard Niebuhr discusses this relational aspect in the language of responsibility—the responsible self is the self that responds appropriately to the actions of others.[3] Paul Ramsey addresses the notion of the right ordering of relationships by employing the biblical concept of the covenant, a symbol indicative of the trusting relationships which lie at the root of all social intercourse.[4] Rules, laws, institutions, and calculations of consequences are important in Christian ethics, but only to the extent that they serve to promote and defend the order of human relationships. Part of the ethical analysis of human experimentation is the consideration of the network of human interaction surrounding the experimental setting.

One way of examining the relational aspect of human social existence is in terms of role relationships. Christian thought has long recognized that different roles involve different kinds of responsibility. The New Testament and the history of the church emphasize that particular "offices" in the church or the secular world entail specific tasks. People are assigned particular obligations by virtue of their social role. Obviously, not all social roles are morally justified, and there are limits to the obligation one assumes in a role, but the acceptance of a particular role does place one under a moral burden that would not be his in the absence of such a role. The Christian church has seldom set out to define what the responsibilities of a particular role are, but generally has added religious sanction to the expectations and functions which society assigns to particular roles.

The physicians in these two cases have undertaken particular responsibilities by virtue of their role as researcher. The role is a justifiable one, within proper limits, because medical research holds promise for human welfare. And although we probably would not hold any individual morally obligated to become a researcher, once the role has been accepted we would probably hold the scientist morally deficient if he did not diligently strive to design and execute research projects that extend human knowledge and serve human health. There is responsibility to do good research, but the obligation to do research is qualified in a variety of ways by other role relations—the relation with a team of researchers, whose opinions and values must be taken into account in designing and carrying out the project, and the funding agency which has its own set of expectations.

But the experimenters also have another very important role, that of physician, and that role carries with it the heavy baggage of a long history of societal expectations. Most important among these expectations is the notion that the doctor is primarily concerned with the well-being of his patients. This expectation is the basis for the trust and confidence which people place in their physician. Thus medical researchers find themselves in conflicting roles. Many feel their dual and often conflicting responsibilities quite keenly as they endeavor to work as investigators dedicated to advancing human knowledge and simultaneously to act responsibly in protecting the health and well-being of the subjects.

This conflict was particularly pronounced for some members of heart transplant teams. It was this concern for patients, expressed especially by the nonsurgeons on the team, that led to the moratorium announced at the Montreal Heart Institute. Indeed the general slowdown in heart transplants seems to be in large measure an expression of genuine concern for the well-being of the patients. By contrast, it is difficult to conceive of any way in which the Tuskegee study can be seen as either arising out of a genuine concern about human interpersonal relationships or promoting such relationships. The role of the researcher seems to have become so dominant that it eliminated all obligations save the single duty to search for knowledge.

The relational aspect is not confined to relations between individuals, for they exist within a social context. As Christians we ought to be concerned not only for individual relations but for the effects of experiments on the public's perception of the medical profession and upon the whole social fabric. Public knowledge that physicians in our society can and have experimented on men like those in the Tuskegee study without their knowledge or consent and to their detriment diminishes, however slightly, the confidence which is accorded the medical profession. It reduces the individual's sense of security, making him wonder whether he, too, may someday become an unwitting subject for a dangerous experiment.

Moreover, focusing too much public attention on an experimental procedure like heart transplantation before major difficulties have been resolved raises expectations in the minds of many people who are then destined to be frustrated when the imperfections of a procedure are revealed. The effects for good or ill of a particular experiment reach far beyond the medical benefits or injury to particular subjects—it affects the ethos of the research and medical community and the fragile structure of the social order itself.

The narrowness of vision which occasionally leads researchers to focus their full attention on the knowledge gained to the neglect of the effect an experiment has on interpersonal and social relations calls to mind another theme from the Christian tradition which is especially significant in the context of human experimentation. It is a Christian concept of sin and the related understanding that all human action stands under divine judgment. The awareness of the human inclinations toward sin should make the individual investigator wary of even his good intentions, since great evil is often done in the name of a greater good.

In neither of the experiments described above do we have reason to think that harm to the subjects was the intention of the experimenter; if harm occurred it was an unintended by-product, but a by-product so predictable in the Tuskegee case as it progressed that the investigators can hardly be excused for their overzealous pursuit of knowledge. The pursuit of good often blinds us to the costs of achieving that good. I would submit that because of the distortion of vision that accompanies any deep commitment to a project, it is difficult to trust the good intentions of researchers themselves to see their work objectively and provide adequate protection for human subjects. Social control of experimentation is necessary.

A second implication of the Christian notion of sin and finitude is the relativity of all human value and truth as it stands under the judgment of God, which in turn points to the virtue of humility. This idea is related in a curious way to the ethic of scientific endeavor. The ethic of science holds that the obligation of the scientist is to search for truth and share his knowledge freely with colleagues so that the general search for knowledge can be promoted. Personal competition, professional arrogance, and deceptive reporting are among the chief vices in the ethic of science—vices which are exhibited all too often in the actual practice of scientific research of all types. Mixing devotion to a worthy task with personal ambition and desire for fame is especially obvious in the case of experimental heart transplant surgery. The attention of the media to this dramatic experimental venture certainly intensified the competitive nature of the whole episode.

In addition to these insights from the Christian tradition, a Christian approach to the problem of human experimentation can be greatly advanced by incorporating some of the methodology of Ernst Troeltsch, who more than most other modern theologians has taken quite seriously the problem of deriving a social ethic from the personalistic teachings of the early Christian church. Troeltsch is most noted, in this country at least, for his efforts to uncover the basic principles that govern the "social teachings of the Christian churches." Troeltsch's essential conclusion is that there is no explicit and intentional social teaching in the original Christian message, which called for individual disciples, not the transformation of the social order; but there are some latent principles with social import which began to be applied first within the church and were eventually extended analogically to apply to the larger society as well. Troeltsch concluded that the primitive Christian gospel contained the seeds of four fundamental social values: individualism, universalism, equality, and fellowship.[5]

A Troeltschian-style argument would go something like this: God loves each human individual and accords him a dignity independent of his achievement. People are valuable not on the basis of any inherent or acquired characteristics, but because they are loved by God. Social distinctions are leveled within the church, since all earthly distinctions are swallowed up in divine love and power. "There is neither Jew nor Greek, there is neither bond nor free, there is neither male nor female: for ye are all one in Christ Jesus" (Gal. 3:28, KJV).

This principle was at first applied only within the church, and admittedly unevenly even there. Eventually the ideas of the dignity of each individual and the equality of all were transplanted into the goals for the whole social order. One of the relevant principles for biomedical research that follows from this dedication to the welfare of the individual is the promotion and maintenance of individual health and the minimizing of suffering, pain, and death.

A corresponding principle in the Troeltschian argument is fellowship or community. All who share a common calling by God are related to one another by bonds which require concern for the body of believers as a whole. Those who acknowledge God as Father must see that all his children are their brothers. Again, this notion of fellowship originally applied only to the community of believers, but the universal implications deriving from the universal love of God ultimately gave impetus to the enunciation of a Christian social ethic.

These twin principles—respect for the welfare and dignity of the individual and a dedication to the general welfare—continue as sometimes complementary, sometimes conflicting principles in Christian ethics. The attempt to balance these two principles in their application to human experimentation leads quite naturally into the discussion of risk/benefit ratios. In the design of an experiment, the perceived risk to an individual human subject must be significantly outweighed by the anticipated benefit to the individual or to society. No experiment could be justified unless it is judged to meet this test, no matter how willing the subjects—even if the subject was the investigator himself. Moreover, the experiment should be canceled whenever it becomes obvious that the projected risk/benefit ratio in fact underestimated significantly the harm to the subjects.

Available evidence suggests that the Tuskegee Syphilis Study failed to pass this test. Apparently when the study began in 1932, no one had any clear idea about what important knowledge the study was likely to produce that could justify withholding therapy from four hundred men. However, it must be acknowledged that the available therapy at the time was less impressive than later treatments, so that the risk/benefit ratio at the outset was less disproportionate than it would be later. But within four years the effects of the disease were becoming obvious, yet no attempt was made to halt the study. By the 1950s, with penicillin as an established therapy, the fact that therapy was withheld in the absence of any obvious and overwhelming social benefit is nothing short of scandalous.

By contrast, in the case of heart transplants the risk/benefit ratio seemed much more favorable for the experiment. Since most candidates for a transplant are in a terminal condition, the primary risk is prolonged suffering and psychological strain, since death usually seems imminent in the absence of some radical measure. Experience demonstrated, however, that the benefits at that stage of development were minimal and most cardiac transplantation ceased. But even assuming a higher success rate, the question whether heart transplant experimentation could produce sufficient social benefit to warrant the extreme social cost in terms of the allocation of scarce medical resources remains an open question.

In addition to the weighing of risk/benefit ratios, a second principle defends the dignity of the individual, namely the principle that no subject should be used in an experiment without his voluntary, informed consent. The principle is obviously a difficult one to apply, as evidenced by the volume of literature devoted to the subject. Pressure, enticement, and coercion make voluntary consent difficult. The subject's ignorance of technical, medical knowledge, and various forms of mental incompetence, hinder informed consent. Experiments in which deception or ignorance is required as a condition of the experiment are particularly problematic.

Yet the importance of the principle remains, as a manifestation of respect for individual rights, and it is reinforced in Christian ethics by the argument that one of the basic Christian values is voluntarism or freedom. In the same manner as each individual has ultimate responsibility for determining his own spiritual destiny, deciding for himself whether to accept or reject the Christian message, so analogously Christians came to argue that each individual should exercise as much control over his own physical destiny as is consistent with the general welfare.

Again, the Tuskegee study blatantly contravenes the principle of informed consent. The men were not even informed that they were part of an experiment. The problem with informed consent in the heart transplant case is quite different. Many of the heart transplant recipients were very well informed—some were taken into the experiment as partners. The question here is whether someone in a situation of desperate illness can offer genuinely voluntary consent. Illness itself is coercive. One of the most serious difficulties of informed consent in cases of this sort is being sure that what is said has been heard, understood, and accepted by the patient. Seriously ill patients so often grasp for any hope, with the result that they often refuse to acknowledge the grave risks that a new, experimental procedure may entail.

Another related issue involves discrimination in the selection of subjects for research. Certain populations such as prisoners, children, the mentally retarded, and the fetus present particularly difficult problems. If there is anything clear about the life and teaching of Jesus it is that he was particularly concerned with those on the margins of society: the outcast, the weak and powerless, the oppressed. There is a tendency for such people to bear a disproportionate share of the burden of human experimentation in this country. It is difficult to avoid the suspicion of racial discrimination in the Tuskegee study. Moreover, it is not unlikely that the presumed immorality associated with the subject's disease may have further dampened normal compassion in this case. This suggests that a more justifiable principle for the selection of human subjects would be utilizing those who stand to benefit the most from medical advances—especially those who have easiest access to quality health care. This, of course, presents the exact reverse of much contemporary practice.

In response to the numerous and serious experimental abuses revealed in recent years, much public and scholarly concern has been directed to the problem. The thrust of this effort is aimed at protecting human subjects from various risks and potential harm. Additionally, these individuals and groups are working toward viable definitions and applications of the principle of informed consent. This last area is especially important to Christian ethics because of its concern for the protection of volunteer subjects, some of whom have been mentally and emotionally disturbed.

In our desire to protect the helpless and unsuspecting, however, we have perhaps paid too little attention to the morally commendable desire of those stable individuals who wish to give a gift of life through the cautious and prudent use of their own bodies as subjects in important and sometimes risky experimentation. Among those heroes are many investigators who become subjects in their own experiments. Such dedication is in accord with the Christian ideal of selfless love. Although the self-sacrificial offering of oneself as an experimental subject would not be deemed a Christian obligation, it could, in some cases, be a manifestation of Christian virtue. This wish to benefit mankind can be especially strong among the terminally ill, who sometimes desire that they be able to give one last gift by permitting some form of experimentation which may help others in the future.

Christian Ethics and Public Policy

Having examined some of the implications of Christian values for an ethic of human experimentation, let us now address the question of public policy. Are the principles which we have discussed solely the property of the Christian church, providing guidance only for the Christian scientist, or should they serve as a guide for all investigators and on that basis for the public regulation on human experimentation? Here, the Christian ethicist finds himself in a very awkward situation. If he believes that his values are rooted in an ultimate reality, he may then logically conclude that Christian principles are ontologically universal and therefore ought to be recognized as such by all people everywhere. But obviously neither the ethical principles nor the underlying assumptions about the nature of reality are shared by everyone.

Should the Christian ethicist then seek to impose his views on a pluralistic society by legislative mandate? History is replete with numerous and unfortunate examples in which religious prescriptions and proscriptions have been translated into law. I would be quite reluctant to impose upon society, especially a pluralistic society, values which are distinctly religious. Our history of religious freedom and separation of church and state rests on the assumption that special religious concerns are reserved for the private sphere. The Christian ethicist should not as a rule propose that "Christian" norms be adopted as a basis for public policy unless they can be justified on larger social grounds as well, that is, by being in accordance with widely affirmed social values.

Interestingly, however, many of the basic values which we derive from Christian thought coincide with the widely accepted norms of our society. Although I have attempted in this article to root the ethic of human experimentation in the Christian tradition, the conclusions are basically consonant with the direction of current philosophical analysis and public regulation. The Christian need neither be amazed or appalled when his conclusions prove identical with those of the humanist. This similarity could be expected, in part because Western humanism has both germinated and developed on Judeo-Christian soil.

Christians have always acknowledged that moral insight is available to those outside the faith. The doctrine of natural law which has been so prominent in Christian history, especially in the Catholic tradition, and the conceptions of the orders of creation in Luther and Calvin and their Protestant heirs are among the ways in which Christians have accounted for the "natural" morality of the non-Christian. What separates Christian ethics from other ethics is not the specific conclusions about any courses of action, but the fundamental affirmations derived from this basic perspective. The Christian ultimately appeals to an understanding of the world and human values illuminated by the figure of Jesus Christ.

The call for establishing general principles and guidelines for experimentation on human beings has intensified because of the increased sensitivity of both the scientific community and law public. Many of the guidelines and principles which are now emerging are secular corollaries of certain Christian values. As an ethicist, I am encouraged by these developments as being indicative of our continuing effort to defend the rights of all citizens. Christians and Christian ethicists must continue to work within the structure of the larger society to refine the emerging guidelines and to assure their consistent application. It is this broad-based interest in the ethics of experimentation that offers the promise of equitable and just guidelines protecting human subjects against harm, without undermining the kinds of responsible research which makes advances in the battle against disease possible.

Notes

1. *New York Times*, July 26, 1972, 1:1 and July 27, 1972, 18:5. For a detailed examination, see the *Final Report of the Tuskegee Syphilis Study Ad Hoc Advisory Panel* (Washington, D.C.: Department of Health, Education, and Welfare, 1973).

2. Renee C. Fox and Judith P. Swazey, *The Courage to Fail: A Social View of Organ Transplants and Dialysis* (Chicago: University of Chicago Press, 1974).

3. H. Richard Niebuhr, *The Responsible Self* (New York: Harper & Row, 1963).

4. Paul Ramsey, *The Patient as Person* (New Haven: Yale University Press, 1970).

5. Ernst Troeltsch, *The Social Teaching of the Christian Churches*, trans. Olive Wyon (New York: The Macmillan Company, 1931), pp. 39–59 and 72–78.

9
Dialogue On Abortion
Paul D. Simmons

In this chapter Paul D. Simmons makes a careful and thoughtful case for dialogue between people who stand at different positions on the morality of abortion. Having addressed the Christian Life Commission Biomedical Ethics conference, Dr. Simmons has written for this book a new chapter to explore the elements necessary for dialogue on abortion.

There is a discussion of the pivotal 1973 Supreme Court decision *Roe* v. *Wade* with attention to the arguments for and against this decision. In order to facilitate dialogue Dr. Simmons points to the areas of agreement between opposing groups. A final section of the chapter looks at Baptist principles which are helpful in deliberations about abortion. The approach of the writer is conciliatory in nature as he demonstrates in his writing the way to move toward dialogue even in the midst of diversity.

Dr. Simmons is associate professor of Christian ethics at Southern Baptist Theological Seminary in Louisville, Kentucky. Having served previously as a pastor, Dr. Simmons is a popular teacher who combines a penetrating insight into ethical theory with the ability to help people make practical decisions. He writes widely in the field of ethics and is actively involved in church and denominational responsibilities.

Dialogue On Abortion

Abortion has been the most controversial, divisive, and volatile biomedical issue debated in America in recent years. The subject is of concern to legislators, women's groups, and families alike. Organizations have developed as lobbying groups on either side of the debate and denominations discover deep differences of opinion within their own ranks. Women themselves are divided on the issue. One woman declared at a symposium on abortion that "Abortion at any time and under any circumstance is murder." Responding to her presentation, another woman concluded by saying: "A woman has the absolute right to control her own body. Thus abortion at her own discretion, and without interference from the state, is her privilege."

Such differences are not easily resolved. Perhaps full agreement on the subject is neither possible nor desirable. However, it is certain that understanding between various perspectives is needed. A syndicated columnist, Andrew Greeley, recently called for a dialogue on abortion.[1] One of his concerns was the fact that denominational cooperation and understandings was being seriously limited because of differences on this issue. His point is well taken. As Paul taught in his writings to the early churches, Christian unity is to be sought through understanding and cooperation.

Elements of Dialogue

Dialogue is a "speaking through," or a conversation between persons of differing perspectives or convictions. Very often getting people (couples, nations) talking together results in reconciliation and a resolution of differences. A more friendly relationship results, based on the fact that the parties now understand the point of view of the other and respect his perspective even if he does not agree with it. Several elements can be discerned in a dialogue.

The first element is a recognition of honest differences. The issues are real and the differences are profound. The New Testament abounds with indications of strong disagreements in the early church, between Gentile converts and Judaizers (Rom. 14), between Paul and Peter (Gal. 2:11–21), the "strong and the weak" (1 Cor. 8; 10:23 ff.), and on the issue of "tongues" (1 Cor. 12—14).

A second element in a dialogue is emotional beliefs. Man is the only creature capable of strongly held emotional beliefs. He is also capable of reason. Debates on issues like abortion usually provoke strong emotions. One lobbyist for legislation against abortion in Michigan pushed a legislator down the steps of a building calling him a "dirty murderer." His emotions had outrun his reason. Socrates long ago laid down one of the fundamental rules for moral decisions: "Do not let your decisions be determined by your emotions." That does not mean you should not feel strongly about your position, but do not simply be a hothead. Reason as well as feelings must be used in dialogue. The head and the heart, light as well as heat, should be displayed. Until people stop shouting at one another and calling their opponent names, no dialogue can take place.

A final element in dialogue is good faith. Each party must grant the other the right to an alternate opinion without labeling it unchristian, stupid, immoral, or other such uncharitable terms. Though Paul disagreed with certain elements in the church he did not use the tactic of branding the opposition as unchristian. He recognized that even Christians have different expressions of their understandings. This is true of abortion, as well. There are sincere Christians on both sides of the debate.

The Issues That Divide

The debate on abortion focuses on two major issues: the Supreme Court (and related lower court) decision and the morality of abortion. Dialogue might be enhanced by outlining the legal decision and the moral arguments.

The Supreme Court Decision

On January 22, 1973, laws on abortion in this nation were significantly affected by a decision of the United States Supreme Court, in the case of *Roe* v. *Wade*. The Court's 7–2 decision held, in ruling on a case from Texas, that laws forbidding abortion except where the life of the mother was in danger were unconstitutional. The justices recognized: (1) the lack of consensus among religious groups regarding the fetus as person; (2) the differences among Americans regarding the proper role of laws regulating abortion, and (3) the difficulty of legislating a solution to the many complex issues surrounding requests for abortion.

Essentially, the Court adopted a compromise position that attempted to regulate abortion without absolutely prohibiting abortion and that attempted to make the pregnant woman, not some other agency, the primary person to make the decision. The Court maintained that the Constitution does not recognize the unborn as persons in the whole sense. (Freedom of speech, vote, and the rights "to life, liberty, and the pursuit of happiness," in other words, are directed to living persons primarily.) The Court then attempted to strike a balance between the duty of the state to protect the woman's right (to health care and privacy), and the unconditional, more limited rights of the fetus.

With regard to the woman, the Court said that her constitutional right to privacy was "broad enough to encompass (her) decision whether or not to terminate her pregnancy." However, the Court added that the state must also be concerned about the importance of potential human life. Thus, the state has the right to limit abortion when the fetus has "the moral equivalent" of personhood.

Following this reasoning, the Court ruled that abortion should be regulated according to three trimesters or stages in pregnancy. During the first trimester the woman alone, with her physician, has the full right of decision concerning abortion. The state cannot limit that choice during the first twelve weeks. In the second trimester, the Court ruled that the state may pass regulations for the purpose of protecting the health of the woman who chooses to terminate her pregnancy. Thus, only competent medical personnel in approved medical facilities may perform abortions. However, during the last three months of pregnancy, the state can limit abortions only to those cases where the life or health of the mother is in danger. During this stage, the fetus has become "viable"—able to live on its own outside the woman's womb. Thus, the Court reasoned, in this stage the fetus is to be regarded as having the rights of persons.

Several things should be noted about this decision: (1) The Court did not rule that women have a constitutional right of abortion, but that they have *a right to privacy* which included decisions about a pregnancy; (2) The Court nowhere said a woman *must* have an abortion for any reason, whether for rape, incest, fetal deformity, or any other cause. The decision is up to the woman and her physician; (3) The Court refused to legislate a single solution to complex decisions during the early stages of pregnancy; (4) The Court recognized the viable fetus as having the constitutional status of a person; (5) The question of abortion is made primarily a moral issue and not a political or legislative issue. Thus, the churches are left completely free to teach their parishioners whatever they wish regarding the morality of abortion and the personhood of the fetus. However, the Court refused to impose one viewpoint upon everyone.

The Morality of Abortion

Whether one supports or opposes the Supreme Court's decision depends upon attitudes one has concerning the fetus and the role of law in moral issues. A summary of the opposing points of view may be helpful in encouraging dialogue. Before there can be harmony, there must be understanding. Before issues can be dealt with, the issues must be understood from both sides.

Opposition to the Court's decision has been led by The Right-to-Life Movement which began as a Roman Catholic organization but now has support from persons of various religious perspectives. Active through local, state and national groups, Right-to-Life lobbies for legislation to nullify the Supreme Court's decision. Basically, it seeks a constitutional amendment that will prohibit abortion for any reason other than the direct threat to the life of the mother. Several bills have been introduced in Congress aimed at accomplishing this aim.

The key elements in the Right-to-Life position can be set forth briefly. The basic belief is that the conceptus is a human being in the same sense that the mother is a human being. Thus, fetus and mother are on a "par"—they are equals—in their moral value and in being persons in the fullest sense of that term. The "life" of the conceptus is regarded as the life of a human being. No distinction in the personhood of the conceptus is made at any stage from the moment of conception to the time of birth. Thus, abortion is justifiable only to save the life of the mother. That becomes a life-for-a-life situation.

A second belief is that the willful destruction of the fetus is murder. To destroy the embryo or fetus even in the first twelve weeks is murder since it takes the life of a human being. Thus, the Commandment, "Thou shalt not kill" (Ex. 20:13) is directly applicable to abortion. Some would argue that the fetus should not be aborted even to save the life of the mother since "better" two deaths than one murder.

A third belief is that abortion should be legally prohibited since it is the murder of a human being. Morals should be legislated and criminal acts should be punishable by law. On this point, opponents of the Court's decision often differ on whether abortion is *always* "murder" and whether no abortions should be permitted or permitted only for certain causes such as rape, incest, deformity to the fetus and threat to the life or health of the woman. They agree, however in arguing that the law should protect the right to live and all property rights of the fetus.

A fourth belief focuses on what are regarded as evil consequences of relaxed laws on abortion. It is argued that promiscuity and irresponsible sexual behavior will result from liberalized abortion laws. Part of the concern is with the effects on the sexual practices of the unmarried. Others argue that couples (whether married or unmarried) may be less prudent in their use of contraceptives and rely on abortion when an unwanted, unplanned pregnancy occurs. Some argue that the Court has encouraged singles to have sexual intercourse since the girl no longer needs to fear the social and personal consequences of pregnancy outside of marriage.

These arguments are frequently heard by opponents of the Court's decision. All of these are not used by every person speaking to the issue, of course, since some argue only one or two points almost exclusively.

Probably the single most important contribution of this position is the fact that it has kept alive the awareness that there is a moral issue involved in abortion. The fact that abortion has been legalized does not mean it is always morally right. The question must still be posed, however, as to whether the efforts to secure a legislative solution are not misdirected. Should the *moral* decision not be made by the woman—or the couple—rather than the courts?

Support for the Supreme Court decision comes from those persons and religious groups who believe the woman and not the state should make the primary decision about abortion. Most of the support for the Court's decision comes from persons who are affiliated with no organization. The Religious Coalition for Abortion Rights, however, is an organization that attempts to consolidate the efforts of various religious groups—Protestant, Jewish, and Roman Catholic—"to safeguard the option of legal abortion." This group does not advocate or encourage abortion but argues that women should have the legal right to obtain an abortion when it seems best to do so. One or more of the following arguments is usually given by those who support the Court's decision.

First, the fetus is not to be equated with the woman as a human being. At best, the fetus is potentially but not in fact a human being. Especially is this true in the earliest stages of pregnancy. Distinctions as to the moral value of the conceptus are often made in terms of the stages of growth during pregnancy. The zygote is the fertilized ovum still in the fallopian tubes of the woman. The blastocyst is the stage of cell division after the zygote attaches to the uterine lining. The embryo is the stage from the second through the eighth week of pregnancy. The fetus is the developing baby from the ninth week to birth. The fetus becomes viable, or able to live outside the womb, about the twenty-fourth week of pregnancy. When that happens, according to this argument, the fetus may truly be regarded as a person or a human being. Viability is the moral equivalent of birth.

The biblical passage that seems to support this view is Exodus 21:22–25 which describes an injury to a pregnant woman who intervenes in a fight between two men. If the fetus is aborted (miscarriage) but the woman is not hurt, then no penalty other than a fine is to be exacted. However, if the woman is injured then the law requires injury *in kind:* "life for life, eye for eye, tooth for tooth, hand for hand, foot for foot, burn for burn, wound for wound, stripe for stripe." This passage can certainly not be used as a justification for abortion since it deals only with a miscarriage. The one thing it makes plain, however, is the fact that *the fetus is not equated with the woman.* The fetus did not have equal rights nor equal moral value. Certainly the act was not regarded as murder.

A second argument is that the rights of women are denied by laws that narrowly limit the availability of abortion. The constitutional guarantee of "equal protection" seems denied to women when more protection is given the fetus than the woman. Some argue that women are denied adequate medical care when they cannot obtain an abortion legally but are forced in desperate circumstance to seek help from illegal abortionists who do not use adequate health procedures. Some also maintain that restrictive laws have been passed by men who have never known the threat and terror of an unwanted pregnancy. In effect, it is argued, a woman is forced to carry a pregnancy to full term against her will.

Studies do show that legal abortions in the first trimester are safer than childbirth. The *Journal of the American Medical Association* reported that, comparing deaths "from pregnancy and childbirth, legal abortion in the first trimester was nine times safer than carrying the pregnancy to term." [2] This helps one to understand the plight of the woman who sincerely feels that pregnancy is a threat to her life. According to the Court, she may now decide whether to continue the pregnancy or not.

A third argument is that the moral issue in abortion should be separated from legislative control. Some argue that the moral question is a matter of personal judgment—those who believe abortion is wrong should not be required to abort for any reason; those who believe it is not wrong should not be prevented from obtaining an abortion (prior to viability). Others argue that the complexity of particular cases (deformity, rape, incest, emotional state of the woman, et cetera) may be so great that an antiabortion law cannot deal with them. Or, the law becomes so complex and cumbersome that the woman is subjected to undue harassment in checking to see whether her case "qualifies." Better to leave the decision to the woman and her physician who together can weigh the issues and decide. Apparently a vast majority (two-thirds) of Americans support this argument.[3] According to this view, those who are trying to pass legislation against abortion are trying to impose their moral views on everyone.

A final argument is the issue of religious freedom. Some church-state groups have sided with the Religious Coalition, not because they or their constituents believe abortion is always right but because they believe in "the free exercise of religion." Laws should not be based upon sectarian or religious views that are to be imposed upon everyone in a pluralistic society. The Constitution guarantees freedom *from* religious tyranny as well as freedom *for* religious institutions. Only the Roman Catholic Church has made official dogma of the idea that from the moment of conception germinating life (fetus) is a human being and equal in value to the woman. The Court ruled that this was a narrowly defined religious dogma that should not be enthroned as law in the United States. Thus antiabortion laws would be regarded as governmental "establishment of religion." One group's dogma should not become everyone's law.

These and other arguments are used by people who favor making abortion legally available. The stress is placed on the woman as the moral decision maker, and on the inability of law to settle such issues for pregnant women or between religious groups who disagree on the value of the fetus prior to viability.

Points of Agreement

There are areas of agreement between the two positions that should be pointed out. These may become the basic building blocks for dialogue on the subject of abortion.

The first agreement is that the conceptus is human. From the moment of conception, the genotype that is established is human. The term *human* is an adjective or a description of the species to which the conceptus belongs. Humans have human fetuses. They are not bovine (cow) or feline (cat), but human.

This means two things: (1) the conceptus is not simply cell tissue that can be regarded as lightly as a hangnail or a wart; (2) the conceptus is not to be regarded as a person or human being until after viability. To be a person is to have social qualities of responsiveness to others, awareness of self, and rational capacities. These capacities require more physical and intellectual development than is present in the fetus before viability. Thus, the Bible portrays man (male and female) as one who is Adam and Eve. They are persons who are born, who have names, and who have a relationship with God based on their rational, moral, and spiritual capacities.

Being human, then, is not the same as being a human being or a person. Every cell in one's body contains one's genetic code—the same code that was established at the time of conception. That genetic code is a human code but every cell in one's body is not a human being.

This distinction between human and human being is important for all discussions about abortion and may lead to fruitful dialogue on the subject.

The second point of agreement is that there is a moral issue involved in abortion. The disagreement is over the proper role of law regarding that moral issue. Good morals require a basic respect for the life processes at every stage in the spectrum of human development from conception to death. Thus, the resolution of the Southern Baptist Convention in 1976 stated that "any indiscriminate attitude toward abortion, (is) contrary to the biblical view."[4] Those who support the Court's decision are often understood (or portrayed) as saying that abortion is right and moral. This is not true. The very fact that abortion is being resorted to on such a wide scale shows that human sexual powers are being misused and abused. This is a testimony to human sin in sexuality.

Even the conditions that cause sexual misconduct are a matter of concern to thoughtful Christians—the exploitation of sex by society, the growth of the pornographic industries, the sex saturation of movies and television, overpopulation, the lack of accurate sexual information, and ignorance or irresponsibility in the use of contraceptives. To this list could be added such sins as gossip and social ostracism that are heaped upon unmarried girls who become pregnant. All these social sins are a part of the abortion dilemma since they contribute to the reasons women feel they must seek abortions. These are sins in which everyone participates either knowingly or by indifference and toleration toward them. Thus, rather than seek simply to forbid women who are desperate with an unwanted pregnancy to have an abortion, the Southern Baptist Convention resolution said Christians should "work to change those attitudes and conditions which encourage (women) to turn to abortion as a means of birth control."[5] Often the woman is the victim of social forces that she neither understands nor is able to control. She should not be further victimized by restrictive laws that punish her while ignoring the true sources of the problem.

Baptists and the Court

On this, as many other issues, Baptists have disagreed. Some are vocal opponents of the Court's decision and actively seek to have it overturned. Others support the Court's decision and groups that attempt to prevent the passage of a constitutional amendment forbidding abortion. In acting on their conscientiously held convictions and accepting "no creed but the Bible," these persons on both sides of the issue are being true to Baptist traditions as they understand them.

At the Convention level, Baptists have dealt with the abortion question in characteristic moderation. In at least two resolutions, the moral dilemma was plainly recognized while the temptation to advocate antiabortion legislation was wisely avoided. Probably the most famous Baptist at the present time, President Carter, succinctly captured the mood and perspective of most Southern Baptists in declaring: "Personally, I am against abortion except under certain circumstances. But I think it would be unwise to seek a constitutional amendment forbidding abortion."

I have participated in dialogues on abortion from television talk shows to conferences on biomedical ethics. Speaking as one Baptist among many, my opinion is that the Supreme Court acted judiciously and prudently in its decision on abortion. While many specific points in the decision might be debated, the overall stance seems entirely supportable by thoughtful Christians. Several principles important to Baptists seem to support this position.

First, Baptists' stress on individual soul competency in religion seems to have its corollary in the stress on personal responsibility in moral decision making. The Court has said that the pregnant woman must make her own decision and bear the responsibility for it.

Second, Baptists rely on the authority of Scripture rather than metaphysical or philosophical speculation or church dogma for its moral and religious understandings. Here the biblical doctrine of man as a responsive, responsible creature before God and the distinction between the fetus and the woman (Ex. 21:22–25) are important. The fetus is important but not as important as the woman. Thus the Court's decision that primary importance is to be attached to the woman's rights seems entirely wise.

Third, Baptists have been strong champions of the separation of church and state. The attempt to enact a law based on a sectarian dogma seems to violate this principle. Baptists insist on every religious group's right to worship as it pleases and to believe what it will. But, with equal fervor, Baptists have resisted any effort of one group to impose its creed on others. This the court refused to do by recognizing the wide diversity of opinion about the conceptus among various religious groups.

A final principle important (though not distinctive) among Baptists is the principle of loving forgiveness. Too often those who zealously oppose abortion speak and act as if this were a sin for which there is no forgiveness. Baptists recognize that salvation is by grace and that God's redeeming forgiveness, not the judgment of law, is the Christian word to every person. Baptist churches need to direct their ministries toward those who seek or have had abortions so they may hear the Word of God's love. This will also involve churches in the attempt to deal with the issues surrounding abortion. Adequate sex information should be provided in a Christian atmosphere, solid guidance should be offered those contemplating abortion, and opposition should be registered against the traffic in pornography and sexual exploitation in the mass media.

Conclusion

Some fellow Christians and Baptists will doubtless disagree with the position outlined here. I would be among the first to support their right to do so. The hope is to be expressed, however, that the discussion will center on the way historic Baptist principles and biblical insights relate to the moral and legal issues in abortion. When discussion focuses on issues, true dialogue will emerge, and the chances for greater unity and cooperation among Christians of all traditions will be greatly enhanced.

Notes

[1] Andrew M. Greeley, "It's Time for a Dialogue—at Least—on Abortion," *Trenton (N. J.) Times*, Tuesday, December 7, 1976, p. A–13.

[2] *Journal of the American Medical Association*, January 31, 1977, reported in the *Trenton (N.J.) Times*, January 31, 1977, p. A–4.

[3] See "Trends in Attitudes Toward Abortion," by William Ray Arney and William H Trescher in *Perspectives*, May/June, 1976, p. 118. (Poll taken Feburary, 1976.)

[4] *Convention Bulletin*, Third Day, page 3, Resolution 4.

[5] Ibid.

10

Genetics And The Control Of Human Development: Some Ethical Considerations

Samuel Enoch Stumpf

The question which Dr. Stumpf addresses is a monumental one: Are we morally justified in entering and altering the genetic structure of human beings? In answering this question, he explores the goals of genetic engineering. Then he evaluates this process from his expertise in theology, law, and medicine.

Underlying the approach of this chapter is a strong belief in the vivid moral sense of society. Dr. Stumpf also explores some of the fears that people have about biomedical engineering.

Dr. Stumpf is research professor of Jurisprudence, Vanderbilt Law School, and professor of Medical Philosophy, Vanderbilt School of Medicine. Before coming to his present position, he was president of Cornell College from 1967–1974. Dr. Stumpf is a prolific writer having published numerous books and articles in the several fields he specializes in. Given his wisdom and charisma, Dr. Stumpf is a leading figure in the field of biomedical ethics. He has delivered a number of major lectureships and is a popular speaker at national forums on biomedical issues.

Genetics And The Control Of Human Development: Some Ethical Considerations

As human beings, we occupy a very special place in the universe in that we are at once a part of nature, on the one hand; and on the other, we are capable of altering the natural order. We are, in short, not only products of the genetic stream, but we can intervene we can manipulate and we can alter some aspects of the genetic structure. In a certain sense, we can create ourselves, not always as either God or nature prescribes, but in accordance with the objectives that we set for our progeny. And we can do these things more and more scientifically. But the question is should we?

The large ethical question is whether we are morally justified in entering into and altering the domain of nature at the special level of man's genetic arrangement. The question might be put another way: Is there a moral equivalent to the legal prohibition against "breaking and entering"? The sanctity of the home, for example, against intrusion is well established. But there are exceptions. We can enter if we have a warrant. Wiretapping is permitted under court authority. This indicates that in the legal realm the Fourth Amendment of our Constitution governing search and seizure is not absolute. Is there a moral prohibition, however, against entering the special domicile of human nature, this genetic structure, and is this prohibition absolute?

Can it be that the really unsettling issue here is that the rapid revolution in molecular biology has forced a new definition of human nature? To be sure, every scientific advance affects our understanding of man. For some, the discovery by Copernicus that the earth is not the center of the universe destroyed a major support of man's sense of cosmic significance. It's worth mentioning in passing about the Copernican revolution that men lost their sense of the presence of God for a rather unusual reason. That reason was that the Christian faith was tied into a nontheological bit of science of that time; namely, Ptolemaic astronomy. And Christianity suffered from a kind of guilt by association so that when the Copernican astronomy was discredited, unthinking people thought that should also discredit the theology. In a similar way, Darwin's theory of evolution seems to some a further reduction of human significance if it were true that the higher species were derived from the lower. And finally even though Freud provided new insights into human consciousness, he radically reconceived the nature of consciousness to the extent that the autonomy of our minds had to give way to a set of deterministic causes.

Following the impact of the Copernican revolution, the Darwinian theory of evolution, and the Freudian reconception of the way we think and what therefore we are as human beings, it would appear that molecular biology is a final assault upon what we took to be human in answer to the question, "What is man that thou art mindful of him?" For the most extreme conclusion now could be that it will be possible to dismantle the primal human matter, discover some equivalent parts in other species, reassemble the selected pieces and bring into being a new kind of person. What seemed very far off in the future is now virtually upon us. And the issue seems to be not only the means being employed but even the ends being sought. What are these ends and what are the ethical problems?

Now before I turn to the three special purposes or goals of genetic engineering, I want to recognize the fear that some of you will have that our knowledge of genetics can be used for questionable and indeed debatable purposes in the area of social control. We are aware of some of the programs that were undertaken in Germany in respect to genetic control. Let me refer to some other possibilities. A very celebrated case was brought to the United States Supreme Court in the 1920s. It had to do with a feebleminded girl, daughter of a feebleminded mother. She was in her own right the mother of an illegitimate feebleminded child. There was a statute in the state of Virginia which provided for sexual sterilization of inmates of institutions where individuals inflicted with hereditary insanity or imbecility resided. Upholding that law, Justice Oliver Wendell Holmes wrote the following words in the course of his opinion:

We have seen more than once that the public welfare may call upon the best citizens for their lives. It would be strange if it could not call upon those who already sap the strength of the state for these lesser sacrifices are often not felt to be such by those concerned in order to prevent our being swamped by incompetence. It is better for all the world if instead of waiting to execute degenerate offspring for crime, or to let them starve for their imbecility, society can prevent those who are manifestly unfit for continuing their kind. The principle that sustains compulsory vaccination is broad enough to cover cutting the fallopian tubes. Three generations of imbeciles are enough.[1]

This is a rather fascinating excerpt from his decision. In the course of this case, the only major defense that could be brought against that state law was a reference to the Fourteenth Amendment which says that no state shall deprive anyone of life, liberty, and so forth. In this case on behalf of the imbecile girl, her lawyers argued that the constitutional inhibition against deprivation of life extends to all those limbs and faculties by which life is enjoyed and under the provision that no state shall deprive us of life, this protection against deprivation includes not only life or survival but also what God has given everyone along with life, including the right to procreate. But that line of reasoning was rejected by Justice Holmes.

While it is known that Margaret Sanger was a champion of birth control, it is not always remembered that her views on this matter were related to ideas of genetic control. Writing in 1919, she said: "All our problems are caused by overbreeding by the working class. . . . More children from the fit, less from the unfit—that is the chief issue of birth control."[2] More recently, Dr. Bentley Glass, the noted biologist and geneticist, said, "In a world where each pair must be limited on the average to two offspring and no more, the right that must become paramount is not the right to procreate, but rather the right of every child to be born with a sound physical and mental constitution, based on a sound genotype. No parents in that future time will have a right to burden society with a malformed or mentally incompetent child."[3] In a similar vein, Professor Herrnstein remarked, "If sometime in the future we find that our population is getting too large and we need to limit it, we could use census information on IQ to decide how and when to limit it."[4] I think we could go on for some time in this vein but I want to turn now to the three purposes or ends of genetic engineering and limit my discussion to that.

The ends of genetic engineering then are at least the following three: (1) to enable people to give birth to a child; (2) to take steps to insure that the child will be normal; and (3) to strive to produce human beings with the finest possible genetic attributes.

What ethical problems are raised by these scientific ends or purposes? First of all, it should be obvious that there is limited agreement throughout society on many ethical questions because it is possible to establish a system of ethics from a variety of assumptions or points of view. Indeed, the reason for the extensive debates in the literature concerning genetic engineering is that there are principally two ways to deal with biomedical ethics. One way is to take a list of principles, rules, or prohibitions and consider them as defining what is right and what is wrong in absolute terms so that a given behavior is either intrinsically right or wrong no matter what.

By contrast, the other approach would give consideration to the circumstances surrounding a given act in which case it becomes relevant, appropriate, and significant to go beyond the act itself and to consider its effects, even the effect of not doing that particular act. This distinction, let's say, between an absolute ethic and an ethic that is more flexible is not, incidentally, a distinction between religious ethics on the one hand and nonreligious ethics on the other. After all, one of the cardinal insights of the teachings of Jesus is gathered up in the saying that man was not made for the sabbath, that the sabbath was made for man, which is a way of saying that you don't start with a rule and make sure that everything is fitted into the rule. To take a life from the first point of view—that is to say the absolute point of view, is never morally justified. If a justification is offered, then automatically one is no longer in the absolutist position; he has shifted to the second mode of moral thought which is some variation of utilitarianism or for that matter pragmatic ethics, or some version of Christian ethics.

Definitions of life, definitions of human nature, definitions of personal dignity—all these can take on absolute or fixed meanings from which only limited conclusions can be drawn and if one does not happen to agree with these definitions, neither will he agree with the conclusions drawn from them. Unless we start with an adequate conception of life, we will find ourselves being forced all along the line to repair our logic and patch up our assumptions. Of course, it would be no better if we simply set forth new assumptions merely because it would make our logic more consistent.

I have emphasized from the very beginning of this paper our conception of the nature of things. I have spoken of man as having a very special place in nature. It is interesting at this point to be reminded that Saint Augustine said there is no such thing as a natural man. You don't understand man until you see him in relation to God. Man cannot be adequately understood without considering man's relation to God. But I do not take this to mean that there is no human nature where it is appropriate for science to function. Put that another way. I would tend to agree with Saint Augustine that to fully understand man it is necessary to see him in the total context. But that does not mean that there is no realm of nature. We can speak of it as God's nature. The question we have to deal with is "How does that bear upon anything in genetics?"

Ideally, what we are seeking is a set of premises which reflect most accurately the real nature of things and which make it possible for us to live and make decisions consistent with our deepest insights and convictions. Such a premise would be that life is a continuum. I suppose if I were pressed I would take it all the way back to Adam—a continuum that does not begin suddenly or at some arbitrary instant. After all, we speak of the transmission of life; and it would follow, therefore, that life is already there to be transmitted.

In principle, then, what we do to life along this continuum has virtually the same effect, almost no matter where we do it. For example, we are able to find reasons for justifying the killing of a fully mature person when we approve the excuse of self-defense. Let me repeat that. We justify killing a man in self-defense. Would it not be easier to agree upon reasons for intervening at other points in this continuum, either very early or very late in particular cases? In any event, it is in the very nature of therapeutic medicine to intervene constantly in the life of the patient, into human nature, into God's nature. Still, the simple sounding objectives of making it possible for people to have children, to have normal children and to produce exceptional children—all these raise problems for both types of ethics, the absolute as well as the more flexible ethics. I want to remind us that it does not follow that if we do not adopt an absolutist approach to ethics that we should then advocate that anything goes. On the contrary, there is virtually universal agreement that the moral sentiment most characteristic of all human beings includes the conviction that we should not harm anyone, that we should not engage in falsehood, that we should not kill anyone. These are negative rules. Don't do this and don't do that. Each of these apply in some way to the three objectives of genetic engineering. But ethics is not limited, incidentally, to negative rules or prohibitions only. Indeed, just as important, if not more so, is the positive duty to seek good. That is the other half of the classic injunction which you see in theological discourse—eschew evil and seek good, avoid evil and do good. Our appraisal of a scientific procedure must therefore rest not solely on whether that procedure complies in a literal way with a rule, but also relies on whether or not the procedure confers benefits upon a patient. The injunction to do no harm must surely mean no more than that the net results should be that more good is achieved than harm, as, for example, when therapeutic radiation clearly does some harm in the process of doing more good. What then is the harm? And what is the good surrounding the means and ends of genetic engineering?

First, there is the objective of making it possible for people to have a child. Virtually every means used by genetic engineering toward this end has this in common, namely, that in some way they circumvent the normal sexual mode of reproduction which is through sexual intercourse by partners in marriage. Artificial insemination by the husband or unrelated donor is a way of bypassing this normal procedure. Is this adultery? And if so, who is the adulterer, the donor or the doctor?

Far more radical as a concept and procedure is the fertilization of an ovum *in vitro* (in the laboratory) and implantation of this fertilized ovum in the mother, or for that matter in the surrogate mother. Even more complex is the prediction by Dr. Bentley Glass who says, "Recent successes in the production of mature ova from cultured mouse ovaries lead me to expect that only persistence by a sufficient number of skilled biologists is needed to attain successful cultivation of human reproductive organs, continuous production of eggs and sperm, and formation by fertilization in the laboratory of as many human embryos as may be wished."[5] And the final step in this direction entails not only bypassing the normal method of reproduction but shifting the gestation of the embryo almost entirely to the laboratory—the gestation not the fertilization. In the common lay press this is spoken of as making test-tube babies. What is the harm and what is the good in all these procedures?

Well, what strikes us first is the deep human desire on the part of people to have a child. The motive for bypassing the normal procedure of reproduction derives from the simple fact that for various reasons this normal procedure will not work in certain cases. One could ask whether it is proper for a couple to want what they cannot have. However, what in principle is the difference between a cardiac bypass operation and artificial insemination? Well, there are a lot of differences—except for life. In one case you save life and in the other you make life possible. But the objection is that artificial insemination, and by inference all the other modes of genetic engineering, is just that, namely artificial, and therefore they violate a fundamental basis of human procreation.

Most people would agree that we can intervene in human biology when it fails, for example, to produce insulin or steroids. But the creation of a child is viewed as something so unique that this event is set off both as special and as sacred. Still, as medical science seeks to fulfill its function of understanding and controlling human pathology it inevitably extends its control to novel areas of man's life. And the new knowledge has considerable bearing upon how we will formulate our ethical judgments.

What is the force of saying that a procedure is artificial? What difference does that make? Is an artificial procedure on that account less good? Or, for that matter, is it even less natural? The test, it would seem, is not whether a function such as reproduction is left completely to natural forces but whether an even more humane result can be achieved. Suppose, for example, that the normal sequence of events is simply random. Is that better or more human than some rational control?

As a geneticist on the forefront of the new knowledge, Sir Peter Medawar has said that:

"A hundred years ago it would have been perfectly reasonable for a married couple to think that the child they conceived on any one occasion was a unique and necessary product of that occasion. That is to say, they would necessarily have the child they actually did have, if they had a child at all. . . . One of the things that has changed is the realization from Mendelian principles that the actual child conceived on any occasion is one in a million possible children who might perfectly well have been conceived on that occasion if the luck of meeting of sperm and egg had been otherwise: So the child actually conceived by any one occasion is conceived as a matter of luck. Sometimes it is cruelly bad luck." [6]

Conception can be random not only in the sense of the chance meeting of a particular sperm and egg but in that conception occurred at all inasmuch as it was not intended. Against this biological roulette it would seem that a deliberate, rational approach could achieve higher human values. But this would not come without considerable cost. If, for example, the problem to be solved is a blocked oviduct, this would require fertilization in the laboratory and subsequent implantation in the mother's uterus. The cost would consist of a series of experiments to determine whether this mode of fertilization and implantation would cause damage or injury to the embryo and indeed whether a normal child could be born through this procedure. Conceivably, some imperfect specimens would have to be destroyed at various stages raising the question whether this is morally acceptable. This would be a morally serious question if it could be held that what was being destroyed was a person. In any case, what is intended in all these procedures is a positive and constructive use of genetic science in behalf of human life by trying to make it possible for people to have a child.

When we consider next the attempt by genetic engineering to make it possible for people to have a normal child, the moral questions take a somewhat different form. It could be argued that medical science has a moral obligation to use its genetic information to reduce human suffering. To be most effective, geneticists must have access to the maximum information consistent with the safety of patients and experimental subjects. But already techniques for determining whether a fetus will develop abnormally are available since through high frequency sound and amniocentesis such pathology as anencephaly, Down's Syndrome, and Tay-Sachs can be detected. It may be that in the future even more abnormalities can be screened, but only after considerably more research, including explorations in the precarious realm of intrauterine life. One way of reducing human suffering is to use this genetic information, as is already the case, to provide an option to terminate pregnancies where serious abnormalities occur. But not every option is an easy one to appraise. Further it raises the moral question of whether the physician should tell everything he knows, which in some cases is less conclusive than his patient would wish. The statistical information about Tay-Sachs babies seems decisive as none survive beyond age five; the quality of life for a Down's Syndrome child has a wider range of possibilities while some babies with severe neurological defects and other trisomies have a brief and tragic span. The very concept of terminating a pregnancy, or abortion, is provocative to many as the supreme violation of morality. Still, in the context of individual suffering as well as the suffering of society, is it not more humane to exercise this option? Again, Sir Medawar says:

"A PKU child may be born in 25 percent of the cases that would be expected if PKU heterozygotes marry. Why should we be victimized by this process of luck? We now have a new understanding of the process of conception and the way luck enters into it. Why should we regard ourselves as morally bound by the laws of chance to put up with the birth, let us say, of a monstrous child if there was some humane and sensible way of preventing a thing occurring:" [7]

Joshua Lederberg insists that it is the geneticists' primary duty to protect the gene pool against damage and he speaks of the crucial need for the detection and "humane containment of DNA lesions (mutations) once they are introduced into the gene pool." Dr. Lederberg argues further that the geneticists' problem is compounded by every humanitarian effort to compensate for a genetic defect insofar as this shelters the carrier from natural selection. In this case, the physician has already become implicated in the question "Who shall live?" [8]

It becomes a moral issue whether society should intervene in childbearing decisions where it is known that parents are carriers of genes which can cause disability in their offspring. It is an interesting fact that between 1930 and 1960 in the Netherlands the frequency of retinoblastoma, previously fatal, doubled probably because a larger number of victims of this genetic abnormality survived as a result of early surgical removal of the cancerous eye only to transmit the genetic defect to their offspring. [9]

The solution to these genetic problems is not necessarily more abortions but more research. At the moment there is considerable moral and legal resistance to certain forms of genetic research which unfortunately results in unnecessary loss of life. A good example is sickle-cell anemia which is transmitted in one out of four cases where carriers are involved. A Harvard medical scientist said recently, "If I could diagnose sickle-cell anemia and thalassemia and other disorders in utero (by doing presently prohibited fetal research) I would be preventing more abortions. . . . We have women who (now) have an abortion because they don't want to risk having an afflicted child. With antenatal diagnosis, I could tell them, three times out of four, to go ahead and have the baby." [10] But the real question here is whether genetic screening should become a regular social policy with the deliberate intention of preventing the birth, survival, or even procreation of predictably abnormal babies. It is also a fair moral question for parents who are aware that they are carriers of possibly defective genes whether they have an obligation to avoid bringing defective children into the world. Parents' rights and interests have to be balanced against the possible pain of a handicapped child as well as the burden to society. Indeed, some children have brought suit against their parents for what they term a "wrongful life" and in certain cases their suit is not frivolous.[11] We cannot account for all the forms abnormality can take nor the different reactions of various parents. Recently a mother in London published in the *Lancet* her deeply moving account of "Having a Congenitally Deformed Baby" in which she described her triumph over the pessimism of her physicians and recorded the thrilling development of her son in his limited world.[12] Here, however, it was chiefly a deformity of the limbs with everything else intact. What about the badly deformed newborns with clearly established diagnosis of incorrigible defects and a prognosis indicating no possibility of attaining minimum human capacities during their inevitably brief life. I see no moral reason why a defined class of malformed newborns whose condition fits the description just mentioned, following carefully articulated guidelines administered with appropriate safeguards should continue to have extraordinary care. Hopefully, we can reduce the number of these tragic cases by earlier detection, cure, or prevention. The scope of the problem of genetic defects for the patients, their families, and for society could become very great. Dr. Herman Mueller has said, "If we fail to act now to eradicate genetic defects, the job of ministering to infirmities would come to consume all the energy that society could muster for it, leaving no surplus for general cultural purposes."[13]

If making it possible to have a normal child presents difficult moral problems so does the endeavor to have the optimum child. What is the optimum child? For some it might be choosing the child's sex. Morally it would be more difficult to justify terminating a pregnancy because the fetus was not the preferred sex than to take

steps through genetic engineering to insure the desired sex. What sex selection would do to the balance of the sexes in the population is not exactly known. But there could be some desirable consequences as we face the enormous population and food crisis. Ability to select the sex of an offspring might reduce the population in places, as for example in India, where frequently large families result from, among other reasons, the attempt to have male children. For others the optimum child would have superior characteristics. Joshua Lederberg suggests that "if a superior individual is identified, why not copy it directly, rather than suffer all the risks of recombinational disruption, including those of sex? . . . Leave sexual reproduction for experimental purposes; when a suitable type is ascertained, take care to maintain it by clonal propagation." [14]
Clonal propagation is a mode of reproduction which is asexual as it does not require the coming together of male and female germ cells. Identical individuals can be produced from a single cell taken from another body; the nucleus of a single cell contains all the required genetic information and can be substituted for the nucleus removed from the ovum.

Cloning may be a long way off since it is one thing to have cloned a frog as Dr. Gurdon did at Oxford and quite another to achieve this with a human. But the experimental momentum is so great that scientists wonder whether it can be stopped no matter what a particular country might do to restrict it. One of the discoverers of DNA, Dr. Watson, writes, "There are already such widespread divergencies regarding the sacredness of the act of human reproduction that the boring meaninglessness of the lives of many women would be sufficient cause for their willingness to participate in such (clonal) experimentation, be it legal or illegal." [15]

One mode of experimentation which would substitute for the usual fertilization process, and which could provide the basis for cloning, namely, the technique of cell-fusion, is not specifically directed to cloning. Yet, cloning would be an additional possibility derived from this technique. It would be unwise and even morally unjustified to resist cell-fusion experimentation if one sought in that way to prevent cloning. For, as Dr. Watson points out, "fusion techniques are the basis of many genetic efforts to unravel the biochemistry of diseases like cystic fibrosis or multiple sclerosis.[16] Moreover, says Dr. Watson, "The cell-fusion technique now offers one of the best avenues for understanding the genetic basis of cancer. Today, all over the world, cancer cells are being fused with normal cells to pinpoint cancer."[17] Therefore, cloning will have to be evaluated on its own merits.

The moral evaluation of cloning must not rest upon the worst possible uses we can imagine to which this technique can be put, such as a dictatorship where super soldiers and administrators would be produced. Nor would cloning be the first nor the most potent instrument at man's command for affecting human life on earth. Positive values can be imagined along with the many disadvantages. But it has always been the case that men have achieved the capacity to do many more things than even an enlightened society would permit.

We must admit the possibility of the misuse, even the diabolical misuse, of power, even the power of genetic engineering. Safeguards and objectivity might not be possible solely within a discipline or even in peer groups. Dr. Michael Barma of Massachusetts Institute of Technology has said, "Self-enclosed peer groups cannot be entrusted with self-control . . . because our educational system does not foster ethical and interdisciplinary values in professional training."[18] We will always face this question "Who watches the watchman?"

The best watchman is the vivid moral sense of society. That moral sense must vigorously uphold the prohibition against harming another person, engaging in falsehood or killing someone. At the same time we can retain the appropriate and necessary flexibility which makes it possible to advance intellectually, scientifically and technologically without losing our sense of the profound meaning and value of life. It could be that we show our highest regard and belief in life when we take seriously not only the consequences of intervening in its processes but also when we take seriously the consequences of failing or refusing to intervene.

Notes

1 *Buck* v. *Bell* 274 U. S. 200.

2 Sanger, M., *Women and the New Race* (1920) quoted in Beckwith, J., "Social and Political Uses of Genetics in the United States: Past and Present," *Annals of New York Academy of Sciences*, Vol. 265 (1976) 46–55.

3 In Beckwith, J., Ibid.

4 In Beckwith, J., Ibid.

5 Bentley Glass, "Human Heredity and Ethical Problems," *Perspectives in Biology and Medicine*, Vol. 15 (Winter, 1972), p. 248.

6 Sir Peter Medawar, "Changing Mores of Biomedical Research," *Annals of Internal Medicine*, Vol. 67 (September, 1967). Supplement 7, No. 3, Part II, p. 61.

7 Ibid., pp. 61–62.

8 Joshua Lederberg, "The Amelioration of Genetic Defeat—A Case Study in the Application of Biological Technology," *Dimensions* 5 (1971), pp. 13–51.

9 "The Changing Pattern of Retinoblastoma," *Lancet* 2 (1971), pp. 1016–1017.

10 Barbara J. Culliton, "Fetal Research: The Case History of a Massachusetts Law," *Science*, vol. 187 (January, 1975), p. 238.

11 G. Tedeschi, "On Tort Liability for 'Wrongful Life,'" *Israeli Law Review*, vol. 1 (October, 1966), No. 4, pp. 513–538.

12 Anonymous, "Having a Congenitally Deformed Child," *Lancet* 1, (June 30, 1973), No. 7818, pp. 1499–1501.

13 Herman J. Mueller, "The Guidance of Human Evolution," *Perspectives in Biology and Medicine* 1, (1959), p. 590.

14 Joshua Lederberg, "Experimental Genetics and Human Evolution," *American Naturalist* 100 (1966), pp. 519–26.

15 James D. Watson, "Moving Toward the Clonal Man," *The Atlantic* (May, 1971), p. 52.

16 Ibid., p. 53.

17 Ibid.

18 Michael S. Barma, "Social Control of Science and Technology," *Science*, vol. 172 (1971), pp. 535–539.

11
Biomedical Ethics
And The Future:
The Response Of The Church
Harry N. Hollis, Jr.

This final chapter considers the church's preparation and response to present and future biomedical developments. It is the theme of the chapter, and indeed of the entire book, that Christians can and should be active in shaping our biomedical future.

A survey is presented of some selected approaches to possible biomedical changes. Attention is given to predictions about the future, the place of the physician in the future, the dangers of unethical research and experimentation, a possible biological timetable, and the increasing temptation to play God in dealing with these matters.

This chapter is written by the book's compiler. Harry Hollis has an active interest in working through the church and through other groups, such as the World Future Society, to help shape the future so that quality, dignity, and fellowship can be enhanced in the human community. It is his view that the fellowship of Christian believers must be involved in every area of society to work for a future that will affirm the life that God has given us.

Biomedical Ethics
And The Future:
The Response Of The Church

He who fights the future has a dangerous enemy.

Soren Kierkegaard

The laser's swift bite, the sonic boom, the electrode charge that can cool a feverish brain or ignite a bomb—all are children of a science that can hurt or heal. How to train them up in service instead of slaughter has become the pedagogical task of our time and tomorrow's.[1]

Throughout this book there have been references to wonderful and awesome biomedical possibilities that the future has in store for us. These chapters have focused on preparation for the future. We have looked at some of the critical biomedical issues about which more and more people are having to make decisions. And we have studied the Christian principles which can help us make such decisions.

In this final chapter a brief survey of some future biomedical issues is offered. In the following pages you will find what some people have suggested about future possibilities in this field. The purpose of this survey is to assist you in beginning to think about what may happen. To be forewarned is to be forearmed. Some of the future possibilities are fantastic. Others are more likely to happen. All point to the need for Christians to prepare themselves to make decisions about these developments.

Speculation About the Future in the Field of Biomedical Ethics

Some look at the future through rose-colored glasses. In an edito-

131

rial about the twenty-first century, F. M. Esfandiary predicts that by
the first decade of the twenty-first century life will be nearly indefinite "with tens of millions of people living well beyond 100 years and
going strong."[2]

Longer life spans, according to the writer, will be achieved
through genetic and biological reconstructions, along with antiaging
drugs, replacements of perishable organs, and the continuous tele-
monitoring of vital body functions. To achieve such an indefinite
existence, the writer predicts that "we will deanimalize our
anatomies, creating durable, modular, imaginative new bodies
adaptable to all elements on this planet and suitable for existence in
space."[3]

One more example of the writer's optimism: "We will be well on
our evolutionary way to a human stage free of pain, free of suffering,
free of death."[4] As interesting as this prediction may be, it is
unrealistic about the way sin enters into human relationships.
Knowledge about ways to prolong life and improve health does not
mean that people will automatically live in peace with one another.
Yet peace and cooperation are necessary if progress is to be made.

The Place of Physicians in the Future

A physician has predicted that in the twenty-first century we will
live in a time when physicians will be unnecessary. In his book *The
Post-Physician Era,* Dr. Jerrold S. Maxmen discusses three possible
medical futures.[5] Here are the three models he discusses:

(1) The physician-centered model. This is the present model of
health care delivery which Maxmen sees as fading into a time when
the physician is obsolete. The physician's present tasks, according to
Maxmen, will one day be assumed by a partnership of paraprofessionals and computers.[6] Maxmen, the physician, concludes about
his profession: "Before the emergence of advanced technology we
had to rely upon physicians; no other viable alternatives existed.
However, computers afford us a new opportunity to rectify the
deficiencies of contemporary medicine."[7]

(2) The health-team model. Medical diagnostic and health treatment teams is a model already in practice to a limited extent.

Nurses, social workers, psychologists, and physicians' assistants perform some of the tasks that were once exclusively the responsibility of the physician. Employed extensively in psychiatry, use of this model will increase in other specialties in the future.[8]

(3) The medic-computer model. This radical departure from medical health care would involve a system of computers to make diagnostic and treatment decisions now made by physicians. A new type of health care professional called a "medic" would provide supportive and technical tasks necessary.[9]

According to Maxmen, computer systems have already been developed to make accurate treatment decisions in the management of severe burns, acid-base problems, respiratory difficulties, radiation therapy, anesthesiology, psychiatric illnesses, diabetes, and cardiac diseases.[10]

Here is a sample of what computers can already do in conducting a psychotherapeutic interview:

Computer—How can I help you?
Person—I don't know.
Computer—Try to tell me something about it.
Person—No.
Computer—Can you elaborate?
Person—I am sick and tired today.
Computer—Do you have any idea why?
Person—Yes, I'm old!
Computer—Please go on.
Person—I seem to have lost interest in everything.
Computer—Tell me more about such feelings.
Person—I have some idea why I feel this way.
Computer—You have?
Person—It seems that I miss having a family.[11]

Maxmen concludes that one day "future historians may finally look back upon the doctor. They may record that despite his archaic techniques, he frequently was a sympathetic creature, intelligent, and at times an ingenuous practitioner. They may recognize that without his willingness to train paraprofessionals and to develop automated clinical programs, a medic-computer model would never have emerged."[12]

These ideas have been presented to show the kind of future that some are predicting. This approach is unrealistic because it fails to do justice to the importance of the personal in the healing process. In the future, we need not fewer physicians but more. Nevertheless, such possibilities need exploration so that we can work for alternatives that use the best technology but also utilize the personal dimension in diagnosis and treatment which the physician is qualified to offer.

Research in the Future

Law professor John Batt has written about the dangers of what he calls "Orwellian medicine," a term taken from the big-brother government totalitarianism described in George Orwell's novel *1984*.[13] Batt warns that some medical researchers and experimenters are already pursuing questionable practices with human patients. He tells of electronic brain implant surgery on such patients as a twenty-year-old mentally ill girl who could thus be prodded by remote control to outbursts of destructive rage in the hope of discovering the source of her disorder. Then Batt wonders if society will decide to use such implants as a punishment for other behavior that is considered deviant.[14]

The future holds the possibility of more brain implants and a continuation of behavior control through the overprescription of drugs. What really should be a concern, according to Batt, is something much worse: "What the avant-garde practitioners of the new medicine have on their research calendars is MAN FARMING. They don't want to waste their time modifying the behavior of patently inferior human beings. They plan to make their own people. And they are serious!!!"[15]

Through the use of selective reproduction by which the sperm of "great" men is used to "improve" the race, through cloning whereby one cell is used to reproduce a complete organism, and through the breaking of the genetic code and the synthesis of life from primary chemicals, such researchers hope to create a kind of super being, an "Overman."

Professor Batt concludes that those who advocate such an approach stifle the freedom of individuals, hamper constitutional government, and threaten human life as we know it. These researchers, he says, "put great stress upon mastery, control, quantification, prediction, precision, scientific ability, and methodical analysis. They care little about joy, play, art, love, literature, family, introspective and deep existential contact with other human beings. Essentially, they are method-centered people. They are definitely not man-centered."[16]

To avoid being taken over by such manipulative researchers, Batt proposes reestablishing the old style medical school under the jurisdiction of a humanist clinician with a separate science research center controlled by one staff. Medical schools should teach students the social and political implications of their professions with a stress on ethics.

The research that still continues in medical schools should be related to patient-treatment techniques, not to cellular and chemical process levels. And there should be liaison between medical schools and research centers. Broad-based committees should carefully scrutinize research that deals with manipulation, modification, and control of human behavior. Hopefully, reforms can come from within the university teaching community but if that is not the case, legislative action must be taken.[17]

Obviously Professor Batt feels very strongly about abusive researchers and he overstates his case to drive home his point. Of course there are many who combine excellence in research with ethical behavior. But, if even part of what he warns us about may become a future reality, then Christians must be actively involved to keep human life from being abused.

Prediction About the Future

In 1968 Gordon Rattray Taylor wrote a book entitled *The Biological Time Bomb.* In it he outlined a timetable for future biomedical developments. Much of what he predicted for 1975 has come true.

The dates he gives are for technical achievement and not for general availability which, as he points out, depend on society.

Phase One: by 1975
    Extensive transplantation of limbs and organs
    Test-tube fertilization of human eggs
    Implantation of fertilized eggs in womb
    Indefinite storage of eggs and spermatazoa
    Choice of sex of offspring
    Extensive power to postpone clinical death
    Mind-modifying drugs: regulation of desire
    Memory erasure
    Imperfect artificial placenta
    Artificial viruses
Phase Two: by 2000
    Extensive mind modification and personality reconstruction
    Enhancement of intelligence in men and animals
    Memory injection and memory editing
    Perfected artificial placenta and true baby-factory
    Life copying: reconstructed organisms
    Hibernation and prolonged coma
    Prolongation of youthful vigor
    First cloned animals
    Synthesis of unicellular organisms
    Organ regeneration
    Man-animal chimeras
Phase Three: after 2000
    Control of aging: extension of life span
    Synthesis of complex living organisms
    Disembodied brains
    Brain-computer links
    Gene insertion and deletion
    Cloned people
    Brain-brain links
    Man-machine chimeras
    Indefinite postponement of death [18]

What does the future hold for man? Professor Jean Rostrand foresees that man will be a strange biped that will combine the properties of self-reproduction without males, like the greenfly; or fertilizing his female at long distance like the nautiloid mollusc; of changing sex like the xiphophores; of growing from cuttings like the earthworm; or replacing its missing parts like the newt; of developing outside its mother's body like the kangaroo; and of hibernating like the hedgehog.[19]

Will Humans Play God?

One who has written widely on the subject of biomedical issues is Leroy Augenstein, author of *Come, Let Us Play God*. In this book he discusses a variety of biomedical matters that must be faced by the human community if we are to have a part in shaping the future positively. Augenstein says that Christians must be actively involved in dealing with problems related to genetic engineering ("Am I My Fetus's Keeper?"); organ transplants and death ("Cancel My Reservation, St. Peter, I've Decided to Stay On!"); population control; mind and behavior manipulation; abortion; and determination of who will be authorized to make biomedical decisions ("Button, Button, Who Has the Button?").[20]

As we look to the future and seek to shape it for good, Augenstein suggests that there we find principles which can be helpful in guiding our decisions and our actions:

1. "There is a basic orderliness in the way things interact throughout the universe." This can aid us in discovery of the facts about our world. Augenstein concludes that there must also be orderliness in human relationships, and he calls for value systems to equip people to make the tough decisions that must be faced.

2. "This basic orderliness was established by a concerned creator." This means that God is responsible for the universe and responsible for the life in it.

3. "Life has a sanctity which should not be casually violated." We must be concerned not only about biological life but also about psychological life. The quality of the totality of human life must engage us.

4. "There is a 'hereafter.' " Augenstein points to the greater scheme of things which must be taken into account when we deal with such matters as transplants or euthanasia. How shall we decide about such matters given the existence of an afterlife?

5. "Agape must be the most important principle governing the behavior of people toward people." We are called to be involved in the biomedical problems people face, seeking to practice the non-selfish concern that Christ demonstrated in his life and teachings.[21]

Facing the tough decisions of the present and the future, "science is literally forcing us to play God."[22] But this does not mean, Augenstein says, that we should be arrogant or callous, as we play a superhuman kind of role in making decisions formerly left to God. Although we must make godlike decisions, we can never be God.[23]

The future requires intelligent involvement which leads Augenstein to this admonition:

Come, let us work together humbly, prayerfully, and above all responsibly as we proceed in this awesome business. For the success or failure with which we "play God" in the next few years will determine whether these are the first few moments in mankind's greatest and most exciting hour or the last few seconds in his ultimate tragedy.[24]

In this necessarily brief survey, we have looked at several approaches to the future of biomedical ethics. Our purpose in this exercise is to demonstrate the urgent need for Christians to get involved in shaping alternatives to a future that might otherwise become a nightmare.

In this final section of the book, we will look at several suggestions for action through the church.

The Church and Biomedical Ethics

As a community of hope the church is equipped to offer help to people struggling with biomedical issues. *Community* is needed in any approach to these matters lest we become so intent on our own profession, our own point of view, our own experiences, that we become too narrow in our outlook. *Hope* is needed to give us direction and the energy that is so essential when we run up against the many complex biomedical problems that must be solved. Here are several practical suggestions for the church to take.

1. Provide educational opportunities to enable people to learn as much as possible about biomedical issues.

The educational ministry of the church can furnish materials to help people become aware of the many problems related to biomedical ethics. Books can be circulated through the church library. For example, the following books are among those that might be included on the subject of biomedical ethics:

James B. Nelson, *Human Medicine: Ethical Perspectives on the New Medicine* (Minneapolis: Augsburg Publishing House, 1973).

Kenneth Vaux, *Biomedical Ethics: Morality for the New Medicine* (New York: Harper and Row, 1974).

Claude Frazier (ed.), *Should Doctors Play God?* (Nashville: Broadman Press, 1971).

Leroy Augenstein, *Come, Let Us Play God* (New York: Harper and Row, 1969).

Michael P. Hamilton (ed.), *The New Genetics and the Future of Man* (Grand Rapids: William B. Eerdmans Publishing Company, 1972).

Harmon L. Smith, *Ethics and the New Medicine* (Nashville: Abingdon Press, 1970).

In addition to providing books, churches can sponsor programs, conferences, or forums to enable people to explore various biomedical matters. Resource leaders from the fields of science and religion should be invited to participate in order that people can learn from specialists in the field.

Study groups in the church can meet together to work through materials on biomedical ethics. One or more of the books listed above might be studied. Or this book might be used as a resource piece, taking a chapter per session to discuss these issues.

2. Encourage Christians to enter professions that are involved in biomedical decisions. Christian biologists, physicians, geneticists, and chemists, to name a few, are needed to work in their fields to make certain that the Christian community will have a part in the

deliberations about our biomedical future.

Take the matter of genetic manipulation. The importance of Christian participation in this field is underscored by theologian Paul Ramsey's warning about the danger of gaining so much genetic knowledge about each other:

Piece by piece of information may destroy our sense that, for all the genetic corruption, God made the world and the human creature and they are good. We may finally lose our faith that under God, life should always be affirmed with joy and hope beyond despair—and lose also our concern that even genetically defective lives be saved and cared for.[25]

Armed with hope and wisdom, Christians must work to see that this does not become a reality. Paul Ramsey's warning must be heeded.

Not only is there a need for Christians to enter professions that will shape our biomedical future, we need Christians to write articles, pamphlets, papers, and books on this subject. Such writing is a natural outgrowth of a Christian faith that sends us out to be salt and light in the world. Certainly the biomedical world needs this witness.

3. Help people think through and develop their method of moral decision making. A continuing task of the church is to assist people in moral decision making. This involves guidance and teaching about what Christians have understood the Bible to teach in specific issues. It also involves enabling people to internalize Christian principles so that they can handle both routine and unforeseen biomedical decisions that must be made.

Through the educational program, the church can help people work through their own decision-making styles. The pastor can facilitate this process in his pulpit ministry. This is important not only for biomedical decisions but for all moral matters.

These questions should be explored: How do I decide what is right or wrong? What resources are available to help me decide? How can I receive guidance and help through the Christian community? What part does the Holy Spirit play in my decisions?

A carefully thought-out method of moral decision making is essential for Christians who must face the complex biomedical matters previously discussed in this book.

4. Encourage Christians to get involved in necessary legislative actions related to biomedical ethics. Every biomedical issue raised in this book is a public matter about which legislation has been passed. Furthermore, these issues are extremely complex and this means there are often heated discussions and strong differences of opinion.

At times Christians may find themselves in different camps on biomedical issues, but it is important that Christians be involved with others in society to shape legislation which will be best for the entire society.

Matters related to abortion, the determination of when a person is legally dead, the patenting of new life forms by drug companies, the desirability of genetic screening, the possibility of euthanasia—all these issues require legislative consideration and thus the active involvement of Christians. The church must vigorously encourage this involvement.

5. Facilitate an interdisciplinary consideration of biomedical issues. Biomedical ethics cannot be handled by scientists alone; nor can people in the field of religion have a monopoly on deciding what is correct behavior. People from various disciplines must come together to share their perspectives. This interdisciplinary approach has been mentioned in connection with other actions but it is so important that it deserves to be repeated at the conclusion of this book.

In order to establish priorities for society, the most careful interdisciplinary dialogue must be pursued. Through its educational ministry, through programs, seminars, and forums, through the writing of books and other materials, the church can facilitate an exchange of ideas between people from all disciplines.

People who claim that their discipline has a monopoly on truth must be resisted vigorously for the sake of society. Theologians, physicians, geneticists, and biologists need each other and they need the input of all disciplines in order to make proper biomedical judgments. They need each other in order to set correct priorities for society. The church can and must facilitate this interdisciplinary dialogue and action.

Christian Faith and the Future

Throughout these pages has run the theme that technical knowledge is not enough to deal with biomedical issues. Coupled with the ability to do things must be the motivation to do things right. To have the scientific technology to shape a better future does not mean that human beings will choose to make the future better.

Christians believe that it is through Jesus Christ that we are motivated and guided to seek what is best for others and for ourselves. Gabriel Fackre says it well:

The Christian faith is future-oriented. Its eye is glued to the screen up ahead on which shines the vision of the world's Creator. Its head has been turned in that direction by one who is himself a foretaste of that dream of a world knit together in which swords are beaten into ploughshares, and man is at peace with his neighbor, himself, creatures, and God.[26]

The biomedical future holds awesome possibilities for us. Through Jesus Christ we have the strong hope that we can not only survive but also help shape biomedical developments for good. For all of us it is a matter of life and death.

Notes

[1] Gabriel Fackre, "Redesigning Life: Scenarios and Guidelines," in *Should Doctors Play God?* edited by Claude Frazier. (Nashville: Broadman Press, 1971), p. 99.

[2] F. M. Esfandiary, "Future Tribute" in *New Times*, January 7, 1977, p. 100.

[3] Ibid.

[4] Ibid.

[5] Jerrold S. Maxmen, *The Post-Physician Era* (New York: John Wiley and Sons, 1976), pp. 5 ff.

[6] Ibid., p. 16.

[7] Ibid., p. 85.

[8] Ibid., p. 6.

[9] Ibid., p. 7.

[10] Ibid., p. 26.

[11] Ibid., p. 27.

[12] Ibid., pp. 264–265.

[13] John R. Batt, "Hippocrates as 'Big Brother': An Essay on Orwellian Medicine" in *Should Doctors Play God?* edited by Claude Frazier (Nashville: Broadman Press, 1971), pp. 125–137.

[14] Ibid., p. 128.

[15] Ibid., p. 133.

[16] Ibid., p. 134.

[17] Ibid.

[18] Gordon Rattray Taylor, *The Biological Time Bomb* (New York: The World Publishing Company, 1968), pp. 204–205.

[19] Ibid., p. 55.

[20] Leroy Augenstein, *Come, Let Us Play God* (New York: Harper and Row, Publishers, 1969), pp. v–vi.

[21] Ibid., pp. 135–139.

[22] Ibid., p. 12.

[23] Ibid., p. 142.

[24] Ibid., pp. 145–146.

[25] Paul Ramsey, "Genetic Therapy: A Theologian's Response" in *The New Genetics and the Future of Man*, Michael Hamilton (ed.), (Grand Rapids: William B. Eerdmans Publishing Company, 1972), p. 175.

[26] Gabriel Fackre, "Ethical Guidelines for the Control of Life," in *Moral Issues and Christian Response*, Paul T. Jerseld and Derle A. Johnson (eds.), (New York: Holt, Rinehart and Winston, 1971), p. 435.